Folger Monographs on Tudor and Stuart Civilization

THE ELIZABETHANS
AND THE IRISH

FOLGER LIBRARY MONOGRAPHS

From time to time the Folger Library plans to publish monographs on significant problems concerning British civilization of the sixteenth and seventeenth centuries. Since the source materials collected by the Folger Library provide one of the greatest repositories in the Western Hemisphere for such studies, the Library hopes to make available a sequence of essays on various aspects of British civilization. Although these essays will be the work of specialists, they will be addressed to the general public rather than to other specialists. For the first volume in the series, the Folger Library persuaded Professor David B. Quinn to write *The Elizabethans and the Irish*. Ireland was of profound concern to the Elizabethans, and reflections of that interest are found in much of the literature of the period.

Head of Turloch Luineach O Neill, 1575. Ink drawing by Barnaby Googe. (P.R.O., State Papers, Ireland, Elizabeth, S.P. 63/45, 60 (II).)

THE ELIZABETHANS
AND THE IRISH

By David Beers Quinn

PUBLISHED FOR

The Folger Shakespeare Library

BY

CORNELL UNIVERSITY PRESS
Ithaca, New York

CORNELL UNIVERSITY PRESS

First published 1966

DA
937
.Q5

Library of Congress Catalog Card Number: 66-11945

PRINTED IN THE UNITED STATES OF AMERICA
BY VAIL-BALLOU PRESS, INC.
ILLUSTRATIONS PRINTED BY ART CRAFT OF ITHACA

To **J. O. B.** *and* **E. E. E.**

Preface

THIS brief sketch of an extensive subject is intended to convey an impression of what some Englishmen thought about some Irishmen and about Irish society and ways of living during the second half of the sixteenth century, and so to offer a sidelight on the literature and history of late-sixteenth- and early-seventeenth-century England. Covering some aspects of the Irish scene which are well known already, others which are moderately familiar to the specialist even if they have not been fully treated in print, and others which have scarcely been explored at any level, its authority is bound to be uneven both in the information it provides and in its interpretations. The author has no expertise whatever in Celtic literature and language; he has not explored the ideological background on which Margaret T. Hodgen published an extensive treatment (*Early Anthropology in the Sixteenth and Seventeenth Centuries* [Philadelphia, 1964]) after this book was complete; he has not used in detail the technical literature of Irish folk life. What it may do is to provide a general introduction to the field and some incentive to more intensive research, if only to remove the many aspersions on the Irish and the English character which some of its readers are bound to discover in it. Although the term "Irishman" is used occasionally to cover any person living in Ireland, it has (with the adjective "Irish") been restricted so

Preface

far as possible to persons from a Gaelic environment, descendants of the eleventh-century population. The older settlers in Ireland, those whose ancestors came from England and Wales between about 1150 and 1300, have been distinguished by the term "Old English," even though, after so long an ancestry in Ireland, and after assimilating so many Irish practices, they might well—and some did—claim to be Irishmen. In failing to deal separately with the Old English, and consequently making the line between them and the Irish sharper than it was in practice, the complex social situation has been somewhat simplified. To have done less would have blurred the ethnological picture presented by English writings on the Irish: to have done more would have required a larger canvas and different terms of reference. The "New English" are those who came in to settle in the sixteenth and at the opening of the seventeenth century.

A by-product of research in other fields, the book was originally prepared as a pamphlet. It has been planned and produced in its present form by Dr. Louis B. Wright, Director of the Folger Library, and by his chief editorial assistant, Miss Virginia LaMar. For the generous assistance of Folger Fellowships, during the most recent of which the book was composed, the author is deeply indebted, as he is also for the thorough and expert guidance which he received at all stages in its preparation.

Much help, particularly on the linguistic side, has been received from friendly scholars in Ireland and elsewhere, to whom thanks is due, which is offered anonymously only because they might not wish to be saddled with the way their suggestions have been used. Professor David Greene, Trinity College, Dublin, very kindly checked the Irish terminology on the proof.

D. B. Q.

Liverpool
May, 1965

Contents

THE ELIZABETHANS
AND THE IRISH

CHAPTER I

Tudor Ireland

THE English hold on Ireland in the early sixteenth century was slight. Royal officials ruled effectively from Dublin over three or four eastern counties—the Pale—in which the landowners and townsmen were Old English settlers of the twelfth-century Anglo-Norman conquest, and less effectively over much of the midlands and South of the island, where Old English magnates, descendants of the Anglo-Norman conquerors, holding their land by English tenures and administering English law, were able to exercise effective autonomy, though from time to time making gestures of obedience to Dublin. Port towns like Wexford, Waterford, Cork, Limerick, and, to some extent, Galway were also linked with the Dublin administration. On the other hand there were large areas in the West (in Counties Galway and Mayo) and North (parts of Counties Antrim and Down) where the settlers had become almost or wholly Irish in language, social custom, and law. In the Pale many of the tenants and poor townsmen were Irish, and the Irish language and many Irish social customs had come to influence the Old English even there. Outside the Pale the Irish influence was greater. Irish methods of maintaining soldiers and of providing hospitality to the lord and fosterage for his children had pervaded many of the settled lordships. Enclaves of Irish under their own lords

1

were administering their own law, through their own judges, under the protection of the Earls of Ormond and Desmond. Irish poets found patrons in the households of the great feudal magnates. The attempt to separate the two peoples had found expression in fourteenth-, fifteenth-, and sixteenth-century acts of Parliament which forbade the maintenance of Irish customs in any of the English areas, proscribed there the Irish learned men and wandering craftsmen alike, and, like most legislative acts not backed by really strong military force, failed to have any considerable or lasting effect. Extending over more than half the island there were purely Irish lordships, quite independent, ruled by ancient families, administering their own Irish laws and customs and making their own alliances and wars. Sometimes they were closely allied with the Old English magnates, and if an Earl of Kildare was the King of England's representative in Ireland, as he normally was before 1534, his allies were also friends of the Crown. Or there might be war between, say, the O Neill, ruler of the greater part of Ulster, and the Dublin government; or else O Neill, with his Irish dependents, might be content with receiving payments (black rents) from Dublin for keeping his men at home. There were border areas, the marches of County Meath, for example, where local raiding and counter-raiding between Old English and Irish was the normal state of affairs.

Henry VIII's officials between 1534 and 1547 had done much to change this. The outlying Old English magnates were made to come into appreciably closer relations with the Dublin government, to admit judges on circuit, and even sometimes to pay taxes, while the growing influence of Irish practices and customs on their lands was curbed though not terminated. Lapsed Old English, like the Burkes of Connacht, were given new titles and agreed to accept some supervision and the enforcement of a certain amount of English law. The range of direct government influence from Dublin was spread fairly effectively over half the island. There, too, the break with Rome was carried through: monasteries were suppressed and their possessions often handed to local magnates to keep them well disposed. A few New English landowners (as we may call settlers installed by the Tudors) were introduced on lands taken from the church or from the Fitzgeralds of Kildare, who had gone into rebellion, 1534–1536. Moreover, treaties had been made with the Irish lords over the rest of the island by which each one of them surrendered some of his independence (on paper). Some took titles—O Neill became Earl of Tyrone. Some promised to hold their lordships in feudal dependence from the Crown—which the Irish laws did not allow them to do, since the lord did not, as in feudal society, own the land. Others simply promised friendship and help in the king's wars. This policy of "surrender and re-grant," and the whole expansion of Tudor influence, had been achieved by installing English officials in control of the government in Dublin, with some English soldiers, backed by subsidies from Henry VIII's English revenues, to aid them.

The Henrician system lacked a really firm anchor, such as reliable local officials could provide, or garrisons of soldiers that could be maintained by local taxes to ward off unassimilated Irish neighbors. Plans to decentralize by having a regional council at Limerick were dropped at the end of Henry VIII's reign. Instead, the government under Edward VI became involved in a desperate military struggle on the western border of the Pale with O Connors and O Mores, which led on, first, to the building of extensive fortifications and then to the seizure and settlement of Irish land, partly by Old English tenants, partly by New English soldier-settlers planted around fortresses on the land. The plantation of Leix and Offaly was carried forward under Mary, but it did not achieve any appreciable success until the early years of Elizabeth's reign. By that time religion had become a new sharp line of division. Broadly, under Henry VIII, the areas dominated by the Old English accepted the

3

Henrician schism; the Irish areas ignored it. Under Edward VI, the first touches of Protestant doctrine, ineffectively introduced, led to a pro-papal revulsion. This, curiously, continued under Mary, where it took the form of resisting English, though orthodox Catholic, appointees to benefices in Ireland. Under Elizabeth, with uniformity and supremacy again enjoined in 1560, the reaction against a Protestant English church establishment crystallized. The churches in the more English areas might be taken over by English and a few Protestant Irish clergy, but the mass of the people remained Catholic and linked with the post-Tridentine Catholic Church. The Old English of the Pale and of the towns put up with rather than embraced the Protestant establishment, and it did not greatly affect their traditional loyalties. In the outlying feudal areas it was a new dividing influence: the Earls of Desmond in the South, at least, moved away from their allegiance to England. Religion was one cause of a series of risings between 1568 and 1583 in which, gradually, the greater part of the Old English aristocracy in Munster destroyed itself or was destroyed. The influence of the government everywhere and at all times depended on the energy of Queen Elizabeth's Lord Deputy and on the strength of his army (which had still largely to be paid for from England) for the time being. The Irish lords frequently ignored their old treaties with the Crown, though sometimes, in the 1560's especially, they entered into new ones in exchange for titles or for security of tenure in the traditional lands of their people. Yet, when they felt like it or were aggrieved by government officials or by their neighbors, they continued to go to war, and the result was the involvement of royal forces, trying to keep the peace by making war, or merely defending their more loyal clients. A provincial council in Munster did not help greatly to extend or even stabilize English power there, largely owing to the Earl of Desmond's opposition. In Connacht, however, there was gradually built up a series of agreements with the Irish which brought a measure of stability and which even provided some revenue for the support of the English garrison. One of the great prob of maintaining any degree of civilization in any part of ...~ country while war was so frequent was that of finding some relief from the continual levy of goods, lodging, and money for the soldiery. Imposed in different forms in English and Irish districts, military taxation in kind was equally destructive everywhere of agricultural prosperity, whether it was imposed from Dublin or by an Irish ruler.

The main Irish area of resistance was in the North. Shane O Neill, a contestant for rule in Ulster who was not recognized by Elizabeth, involved the Crown in intermittent fighting from 1560 to his death in 1567. His successor, Turloch Luineach O Neill, equally unrecognized by the Queen, proved much more skillfully flexible, provoking English intervention by his independence and at the same time evading its more serious consequences. Attempts to settle New English colonists in Antrim and Down, on the fringes of the O Neill sphere of influence, failed in the 1570's, and the attempt to install them merely acted as an irritant. Hugh O Neill (Aodh Ó Néill), Baron of Dungannon and, from 1587, Earl of Tyrone, was set up, after an English education, to act as a check on Turloch. He did so and finally succeeded Turloch but once he was in the saddle built up his own military machine, relying on both English and Irish methods. In this way he could gradually resist English encroachments on his borders, in Monaghan, in Down and Antrim, Armagh, Fermanagh, and Donegal, where sheriffs, garrisons, and even a few landowners were being pushed forward and his family's old dependents were being detached. Finally, in 1594, he made his break with the Queen and in 1595 assumed the title of O Neill on Turloch's death. For four years he held Elizabeth's forces in check by a combination of war and diplomacy. Then, failing to get his widening claims to autonomy accepted, he gradually set the greater part of Ireland on fire. In Munster he worked on the Irish and Old English, who had lost much land and power to New English settlers after 1583, so that they rose

5

in revolt in 1598. Similarly, in Connacht, he gradually played, with success, on local apprehensions of the ultimate effects of English victory. He found allies along the borders of the Pale, and even a handful of the Old English there joined him.

There was some measure of unity against England over most of the island, but it was scarcely a national unity. Religion gave the movement such cohesion as it had. Catholicism was now on the offensive, and opinion in most parts of Ireland had hardened against the toleration of state Protestantism. Papal encouragement and the work of missionary Jesuits had done something; the existence of the Anglo-Spanish war from 1585 onward did more; but Philip II, in his caution, did almost nothing for his potential Irish allies. When Philip III sent a force to Kinsale in 1601, it was too late: English power was again reviving, while the help sent was in any case too small. Behind the religious issue there was the feeling on the part of the Irish lords, individually and collectively, that if they did not resist the English armies successfully, now that large-scale war had begun, their old native polity would be replaced finally and forever. This held O Neill in the field until he submitted on March 28, 1603, after, indeed—though he did not know it—Queen Elizabeth, who symbolized all that aggressive English nationalism meant to him, had died.

In 1566 Thomas Lancaster, Protestant Bishop of Kildare, had told Queen Elizabeth, "This poor realm may by your Grace be brought to good order, and it shall be especially a fame immortal that it was brought about by the hand of a woman." [1] Neither sender nor recipient can have realized that it would take nearly forty years of intrigue and fighting, the loss of much that was valuable in Irish society, besides the expenditure of many Irish and English lives and vast quantities of English money, before an English "order," under the aegis of a Scottish king, could be freely imposed upon the island.

CHAPTER II

England over All

How and out of what materials England invented her cultural nationalism has been very inadequately explored by her historians. One decisive element in it was her attitude to non-English elements outside. Most expanding states have adopted attitudes of conscious superiority toward other peoples in their path whom they deigned to conquer. Since, normally, the expansion of European states in the early modern period was into Muslim, Hindu, or pagan areas, the superiority could be most easily expressed in the contempt of Christian for infidel, though, of course, it might also be expressed in terms of means for war making or of material civilization. The inhabitants of those parts of the British Isles in the later Middle Ages who were outside, or ineffectively within, the English state were Christians. They were, in color and in physique, not notably distinct from Englishmen. They had a civilization of their own but one which had been touched, at least, and modified, in part, by the same waves of Norman conquerors that had built up England as an effective political society, a state.

Yet the English attitude to Welsh and Scots and Irish had in it a good measure of national pride. It is not easy to analyze its constituents. It has much to do with the ascendancy of the English language. This was the symbol of the success of the Anglo-

Saxon population of eleventh-century England in turning Normans into more than English Englishmen. It is seen too in the triumph of Anglo-Saxon over Norman influence in Lowland Scotland, even though the people there, as members of a Scottish kingdom, remained in English eyes something less than Englishmen. It is illustrated in Ireland by the establishment of an English outpost out of the conquests of the Anglo-Norman adventurers of the twelfth century, though in the latter case English speech had scarcely ousted Norman-French before it was endangered by the resurgent Gaelic tongue.

The English outlook had also much to do with inherited attitudes about land. A stable land system, anchored by primogeniture, fitted the wheat- and vine-growing areas, the beer- and wine-drinking zone, of continental Europe and the English Lowlands. The pastoral society of the western highlands and coast lands, with oats and barley grown where possible and with a milk- and whiskey-drinking tradition, was more flexible in its arrangements about land and was consequently looked down upon as being primitive and savage. This attitude is concerned also with the monarchy and its pattern of government from the center, which fixed the core of Englishness firmly in the Southeast—where it has remained.

The intensity of the attitude of superiority did not depend so much upon material or even ideological differences between the English and non-English areas as on discrimination between those non-English areas which had most or least easily accepted English institutions or English rule. Consequently, their willingness to accept English rule, and all the major socio-agricultural customs that went with it, was the main criterion for the acceptance or rejection of the non-English groups. Such an indication of attitudes, without intensive research in a difficult field, bristling with subjective obstacles, must necessarily be imprecise, yet to start as writers have tended to do in the past in terms of "good"

English and "bad" Irish, or the reverse, according to the stand-point of the writer, or his location on one side or the other of the Irish Sea, is clearly useless.

The differentiation of English attitudes can be seen very effectively in the Tudor period. Part of Wales had already been fully absorbed under English government before 1485: by 1547 the remaining partly Anglicized areas had become wholly so in law, administration, and land tenure, and this without fighting. Elizabethan attitudes toward the Welsh were superior, contemptuous in a condescending though sometimes friendly way. The Welshman held on to his language in spite of official discouragement; he drove his cattle untidily across England to the London market; he sounded like a foreigner even when he spoke English; he was given, in English eyes, to thievery, gluttony, and poverty. Yet Welshmen bent before the English rather than faced them. Except for a handful of Catholic refugees, Wales did not resist Tudor authority. At the same time, under the shelter of their language and their rural dispersal, the Welsh retained many elements of their traditional culture. They might in their own way despise the English and the ultra-Anglicized Welshman, but they were almost always able to outwit them.

Toward the Scots, English attitudes were ambivalent. On the one hand, there seemed to be much flattery by imitation. Scotland appeared to have created much of the fabric of an English state. She was engaged in spreading the English language and, it seemed, culture amongst the Gaelic-speaking barbarians in the West and North. Tudor England helped Scotland to establish her Protestant religion, which was more English than Continental in its final shape, and she flooded her with publications and other cultural propaganda, while all the time looking forward either to her conquest or absorption.

Toward Ireland, English attitudes were most complex of all. If we ask what the English would have desired to create in Ireland, provided there had not been, as there was not in Wales, any continuing armed opposition, the answer is something like this:

A landowning class robbed of all special privileges as against the Crown, disarmed, and preferably containing no really powerful magnates.

A church whose property was at the disposal of the state and whose clergy were willing to act as instruments of royal policy.

A uniform system of jurisdiction on English lines, with perhaps a fair range of local variation, together with a system of universal taxation based mainly in landed property, without precluding the representation of landowners and the more wealthy merchants in a not very powerful parliament.

A stable population from which movement of individuals or groups, either seasonal or professional, had been virtually eliminated by coercion and by the cooperation of the land-owners.

The maintenance throughout the country of a network of officials of the central administration, assisted as long as was desirable by garrison troops, though gradually turning over some functions of local government to a passive landowning class which was itself capable of imposing social peace by repressive means but which would not turn against the Crown.

The establishment of English as the sole official language.

Some of these were objectives of Tudor monarchs and statesmen in England which they were never able fully to realize there, and, we may well remember, in all the plethora of schemes for "civilizing" Ireland, that the techniques and resources of sixteenth-century governments were severely limited and fell far short of their aspirations. It is consequently not surprising that before 1603 no decisive successes in the Anglicizing program had been won.

Ireland, and the societies of the Old English and native Irish alike, did not fit these requirements. On the one hand, the feudal elements, notably in the great earldoms of the South, were much too unruly and had, in virtue of the continued intransigence of the Irish rulers and the possibility of alliance with them, a genuine alternative to conformity—under, however, the threat of ultimate destruction, as happened in the earldom of Desmond, of their whole society. Secondly, the Irish areas were at once too different and their rulers too flexible in their resources for a policy of complete submission to be enforceable. The social lines were drawn, almost invariably, across the English criteria of civilization and good order. Rules of descent in their offices and in land contravened the habit of primogeniture (and its correlative of escheat). The hereditary status of the learned class, and the mobile character of some of its members and of certain ancillary craftsmen and specialist groups, appeared disruptive of the influence of the state and of the policy of stabilizing the population. The creation of small, stable, landowning units was difficult to reconcile with extensive grazing rights and summer transhumance, which involved a certain undesirable diffusion of property rights. The continued emphasis on cattle as stock and cattle as wealth made more difficult a neat rearrangement of tenancies inside the landowning units and represented an undesirable degree of specialization in agricultural production, which state taxation required to be diversified. Finally, though the state could take over much church property and formally install obedient clergy (having given away monastic property as rewards to its own officials and to landowners alike), it could not make the Irish accept new forms of service and new articles of belief which were wholly identified in language and content with the Anglicizing process; and to distaste for English Protestant innovation was added the influence of the positive Catholicism of the Council of Trent, which increasingly found a response on the Irish side. Finally, as so often happens in the intensification of an old, long-drawn-out struggle, bitterness, mistrust, mutual treachery, and cruelty made a long-term reconciliation increasingly difficult or even impossible, so that no new restatement of the political relationship between English and Irish was achieved.

Irish pride, the English saw as an obstacle to the civilizing of the country: English pride, Irishmen were sure, made them go blindly on with the conquest of the country.

An Irish writer attacking the English in 1578 said:

And further they are the greatest murderers and the proudest people in all Europe and I am surprised that God tolerates them so long in power—except that He is long-suffering and that His avenging hand is slow but sure, and, besides, that the Irish themselves are bad, and that this misfortune is to chastise and correct them. I shall say no more, because I should use up all my ink and paper on this subject.[1]

Hard and bitter words were not the monopoly of one side or of the other.

Francis Bacon had little sympathy for Irish social customs, which he did not consider it necessary to preserve, but his attitude toward the Irish was, nonetheless, a cool and rational one. He saw, above all, that the continuance of an attitude of superiority by the English toward the Irish—and of preference to the Old English inside Ireland—could never bring any real reconciliation. A long-range policy must treat both as equals. Thus he wrote to Cecil in 1602:

The keeping of the principal Irish persons in terms of contentment, and without cause of particular complaint, and generally the carrying of an even course between the English and the Irish, whether it be in competition, or whether it be in controversy, as if they were one nation (without that same partial course which hath been held

12

by the governors and counsellors there, that some have favoured the Irish and some contrary) is one of the best medicines of state.[2]

Throughout the Tudor period doubts remained whether the Irish could ever be reformed into an English pattern. A writer in 1601, sensitive that southern Europeans regarded the English, so he said, as "simple, uncircumspect, unwary, easy to be deceived and circumvented by them," thought that English ways might nonetheless be taught to outsiders from the less fortunate parts of Great Britain: "We may daily perceive in our own country wherein our Northern and Welshmen, when they come to London, are very simple and unwary, but afterward by conversing a while and by the experience of other men's behaviors, they become wonderful wise and judicious." [3] No such hope was expressed about the Irish.

CHAPTER III

Old Ireland

THE society of Gaelic Ireland was the largest remnant of that old Atlantic coastal society which had first emerged several millennia earlier and which had maintained itself in some degree even in the sixteenth century in the lands between northwestern Iberia and Norway.[1] Ireland and the Western Highlands of Scotland were the two areas where it had remained strongest and where it had been affected only marginally by the continental society of the European lowlands, which had spread into England in successive waves, first with the Romans and later with their barbarian successors, and had reached Ireland only in the twelfth century. Even there it had been turned back and the Irish polity largely reconsolidated in the fourteenth and fifteenth centuries.

The basis of Irish society was mainly pastoral, with cattle as its chief source of wealth and its symbol of prestige. It was also a seafaring society, with a coastal fishing and seafood exploiting tradition which was a significant part of its economy. Its agriculture was based on oats rather than wheat, and it used at least part of its grain for winter cattle feed. One of its characteristic features was its transhumance, a movement with flocks and herds into summer pastures while the oats was growing, with the establishment there of a summer encampment (the booley, *buaile*) for the greater part of the population. Settlement was concentrated not in towns or large villages but either in small irregular rural units or in individual farmsteads. The latter, when they were those of local rulers, were often themselves considerable clusters of settlement. But there were few buildings of any great size or stability: mud and wattle, timber, turf, and straw were sufficient, apart from the strong stone walls, usually circular, which enclosed some of the farmsteads and made primitive fortresses of them, or the tall tower castles which sprang up in the fourteenth and fifteenth centuries as symbols of resistance to the Old English settlers.[2]

The unit of political authority was small. The *tuath* was not usually more than 300 or 400 square miles in extent, and yet its ruler regarded himself as sovereign. He was almost certainly linked with a superior ruler, unless he was one himself, by bonds of fealty and tribute. These larger groupings might still be quite small, and they, in turn, would probably be knit into a provincial grouping under, say, O Neill in the North or O Brien in the West. Such provincial rulers could issue ordinances of limited scope inside their own particular *tuath*, but they had no powers of general legislation over their client states. Inside their own *tuath*, too, the rulers moved from place to place, being entertained (in lieu of taxation) by the freemen, who were usually a depressed class, only less so than the serfs whom they still retained in some numbers under them.

Old Irish society had taken to war largely as a sport—this aspect was maintained in the cattle raids still carried on largely for reasons of prestige. But the revival of Irish influence in Ireland between the thirteenth and fifteenth centuries had been achieved largely by the development of a professional soldiery.[3] The backbone of this was the galloglass. Hereditary galloglass (*gallóglaigh*) families were imported originally from western Scotland and settled in many of the *tuatha* as heavily armed infantrymen, equipped with armor, powerful swords, and long-handled axes. To maintain them and their attendants and to second them with bands of more lightly armed infantry, kerns (*ceithearnaigh*) were maintained by the system of bonaght (*buannacht*), a levy of food, drink, and cash payments for the upkeep of the soldiery. This was the system which, when superadded to the feudal arrangements of the Old English lordships, was known as coyne and livery. It imposed heavy burdens on Irish society, chiefly on the freemen farmers, and it tended to exalt the power of the rulers, more especially of those provincial kings who commanded the services of a large number of soldier-maintaining clients. Below the rulers it enhanced the prestige and strength of the soldiery.

The ruling families in the Irish *tuatha* were old and proud.[4] They handed down their authority not from father to eldest son but from the head of a family group (*deirbhfhine*) to the next strongest personality in the group. A ruler might nominate a successor (*tánaiste*) in his lifetime, and he could usually gain the support of the rest of the family. If there was no tanist, the successor emerged from the family by election or force of arms, the latter being only too frequent and a cause of weakness in the whole polity. Lands, too, descended in a smaller family group (*geilfhine*), and there could be a certain amount of repartitioning at a succession. No landholder could alienate landed property without the consent of the family group as a whole.

Law was traditional: custom was the dominant influence on life. There was a very strong sentiment on the side of local autonomy and against any degree of government from a distance. Armed robbery across land borders and along the coasts was not unusual. There was a tendency for the ruling families to gain more authority and to build up the power of their own relatives by assigning lands to them where old families had died out. The superior kings were also tending to exercise some direct authority over their clients. Yet by the second half of the sixteenth century there was still much fluidity in the local administration of

Irish principalities and also a fair measure of resilience. Lacking the encumbrance of towns, guarded by woods and bogs and mountains, and retaining much mobility, Irish communities were hard to dominate.

The professional men of Irish society ranked as part of the aristocracy of the Irish *tuatha.* The brehons (*breitheamhain*) were hereditary jurists, holding land as the judges of the principality and transmitting their offices in their family. They trained their successors, by the study of archaic texts and unrealistic commentaries, to believe in the doctrine of the immutability and uniformity of Irish law. They operated as a factor working against positive legislation by the ruler, and, by their professional associations with other jurists, they helped to prevent radical divergences in the working of the legal system from *tuath* to *tuath.* The law was based primarily on fines, not physical punishment, for criminal offenses, and on arbitration for civil disputes: it was practical and, admitting the prestige of the jurists, effective in spite of its archaic flavor, but not at all an efficient instrument for the enhancement of the power of the ruler or the state

The poets (*filidh*), too, formed a privileged order, with many grades within it.[5] Their task was to gratify the local rulers by song, recitation, and story, especially in the form of panegyric or of satire on their enemies. Some were landed and stabilized at a particular court (or it might be in the retinue of an Old English settler magnate), but a poet might set out on a wandering life and—as some inferior grades did, in any event—hawk his skills from lord to lord. The poets, also, were reared in hereditary lore of an archaic character, usually in peripatetic schools. The academic character of their learning did not prevent them from expressing themselves strikingly, though they did so in rigorous metrical forms and in old-fashioned language. In addition they were, as Professor David Greene has said, "by the very nature of their calling . . . the paid propagandists of the existing order of

17

things." [6] One might say that it was traditional with them, almost a duty indeed, to attack all things English in their defense of the Irish society in which they were a favored group. Yet some of them were patronized by Old English nobles who came to like both their verses and their flattery. A few were cynical enough to admit that they changed the objects of their satire as they moved across the cultural divide.

Irish medicine, too, was handed down in landed families maintained for that purpose in most principalities.[7] Also privileged, they had their own hereditary body of medical lore, but that which was purely traditional has been largely lost to us. Current between the fourteenth and the sixteenth centuries were Irish versions of the texts of the twelfth-century European renaissance—Galen, Avicenna, and Hippocrates—which soon subsided into an academic formalism as unrealistic as the law tracts. Although these writings were taken seriously as theory, they nevertheless do not seem to have interfered too drastically with the empirical practice of medicine and surgery. The medical schools also seem to have been peripatetic, aspirants from medical families following a master or group of masters as they moved around a circle of their clients.

Lesser freemen—jesters, gamblers, musicians, and craftsmen like tailors, woodworkers, smiths, and armorers—were usually itinerant, as were such merchants as were to be found—though these were likely to be Old English traders from the towns.

The learned classes were wedded to the existing Irish social system, although the fact that brehons could administer Irish law to Irish enclaves in the territories of the Earls of Desmond and Ormond, and that poets could compose eulogies to such Old English feudal families, shows that their allegiance was not entirely immutable. The freedom of movement and the prestige which the poets enjoyed and which they shared with lesser entertainers and craftsmen was one of the things they stood to lose in a fully Anglicized state.

In such a society it might be possible to obtain a generalized (and temporary) loyalty to an outside authority. He could possibly be an English king—Richard II and Henry VIII both aspired to be such—or else a king's representative who was a great figure in his own right, like Richard, Duke of York, or an Old English magnate who was also regarded as an Irish ruler, like the eighth Earl of Kildare. But such an allegiance was most likely to be personal and transient only: it could scarcely be institutionalized. Thus it was not easy to see how the Irish polity could be brought permanently within the bounds of a centralized state.

CHAPTER IV

The Curious Eye

With English attitudes of superiority there was often combined an intense degree of curiosity. In Queen Elizabeth's reign, Ireland appears in English ballads, on the stage, in the verse of several leading poets, in prose newsletters, in promotion pamphlets for colonization, in royal proclamations, in descriptive treatises and in historical narratives, and, most voluminously, in English state papers.[1] She is fully, if unevenly, represented; her faults and misdeeds are stressed more than her more positive qualities; but she is constantly present in the English consciousness. The earliest stages of contact between Englishmen and non-English cultures were likely to be governed by the desire to define and limit their inferiority (or non-Englishness) and to find ways of forcing them into a new English pattern, reforming them or obliterating them. But beyond that there was the tendency to observe alien cultures for their own sake. The making of notes, the taking an interest—scornful or superior, earnest or objective—led from casual observation to some measure of systematic study of Irish life and Irish society, to an elementary ethnology, if not precisely to social anthropology. Just as modern students of North American Indian tribes summarize their knowledge of distinctive characteristics under lists of culture traits, so English observers compare Irish traits with those of

Plate 1. Map of Ireland about the middle of the sixteenth century. By Robert Dunlop.

Plate 2. Irish galloglasses and their attendants, 1521. Pen and wash drawing by Albrecht Dürer. (Berlin Cabinet of Engravings, colored copy in National Gallery of Ireland, Dublin.)

DRAVN AFTER THE QVICKE

Plate 3. Irish kern, ca. 1540–1550. Woodcut; artist and engraver unknown. (Ashmolean Library, Oxford.)

Plate 4. Irish kern, woman, and young piper. Water-color drawing, ca. 1575, by Lucas de Heere, after a lost drawing by the artist of Plate 3. (University Library, Ghent, MS. 2466.)

Plate 5. Irish kern and old man (with two women from Old English areas). Water-color drawing by Lucas de Heere, ca. 1575, after a lost drawing by the artist of Plate 3. (British Museum, Additional MS. 28330.)

Plate 6. Irish beggar (with a woman from the Old English Pale). Water-color drawing by Lucas de Heere, ca. 1575, possibly after a lost drawing by the artist of Plate 3. (University Library, Ghent, MS. 2466.)

Plate 7. An Irish lackey. (Album of Hieronymus Tielch, ca. 1603–1606. Henry E. Huntington Library, MS. HM 25863.)

Plate 8. One of O Neill's soldiers (possibly an O Cahan), ca. 1600. (Reconstruction of the Dungiven costume, see *Ulster Journal of Archaeology,* 3rd ser., vols. XXIV–XXV [1962], pp. 119–142, plates XIII–XVI.)

Plate 9. Irishwoman picking lice from the head of a kern. Woodcut; artist and engraver unknown. Andrew Boorde, *The fyrst boke of the introduction of knowledge* [1548?].

Plate 10. An Irish kern, Rory Og O More, ca. 1575. Woodcut, probably by John Derricke. John Derricke, *The Image of Irelande* (London, 1581).

Plate 11. An Irish lord prepares to set out on a cattle raid, ca. 1575. Woodcut, probably by John Derricke. John Derricke, *The Image of Irelande* (1581).

Plate 12. An Irish lord (MacSweeney) dines in the open air, ca. 1575. Woodcut, probably by John Derricke. John Derricke, *The Image of Irelande* (1581).

Plate 13. An Irish cattle raid. Woodcut, probably by John Derricke. John Derricke, *The Image of Irelande* (1581).

Plate 14. English counterattack on Irish cattle raiders. Woodcut, probably by John Derricke. John Derricke, *The Image of Irelande* (1581).

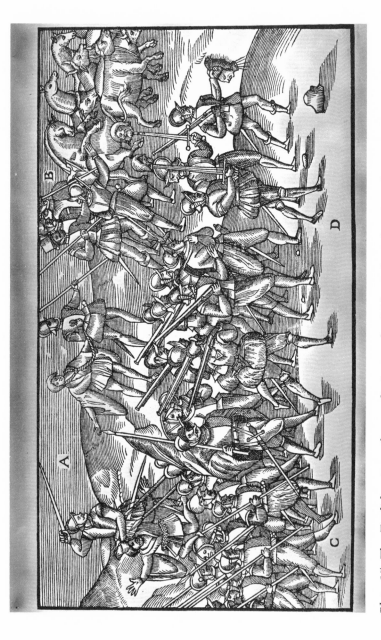

Plate 15. The English return after retaliation on the Irish cattle raiders. Woodcut, probably by John Derricke. John Derricke, *The Image of Irelande* (1581).

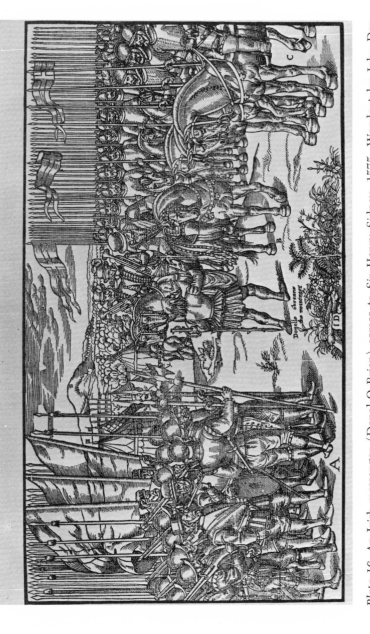

Plate 16. An Irish messenger (Donal O Brien) comes to Sir Henry Sidney, 1575. Woodcut by John Derricke. John Derricke, *The Image of Irelande* (1581).

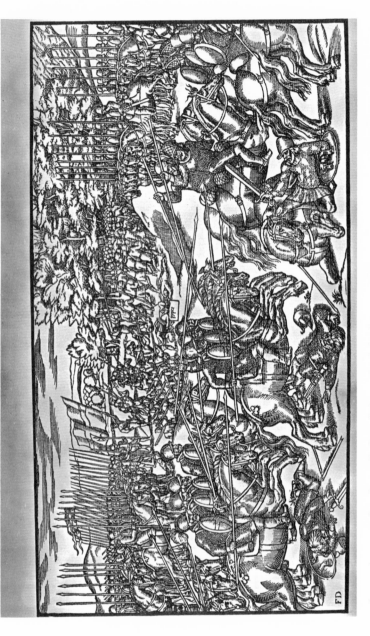

Plate 17. A cavalry skirmish (English on the left; Irish on the right). Woodcut, probably by John Derricke. John Derricke, *The Image of Irelande* (1581).

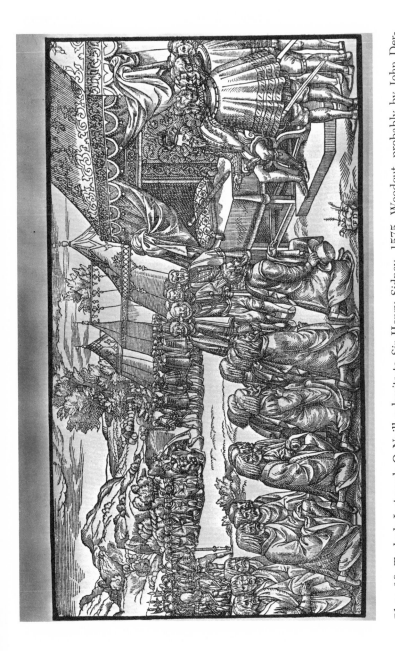

Plate 18. Turloch Luineach O Neill submits to Sir Henry Sidney, 1575. Woodcut, probably by John Der-ricke. John Derricke, *The Image of Irelande* (1581).

Plate 19. Captain Dowdall and his Irish boy (at Ballyshannon, 1593). Pen and wash drawing by John Thomas, 1593 (detail). (British Museum, Cotton MSS., Augustus, II, 38.)

Plate 20. Irish horsemen, galloglasses, and kern in retreat (Ballyshannon, 1593). Pen and wash drawing by John Thomas, 1593 (detail). (British Museum, Cotton MSS., Augustus, II, 38.)

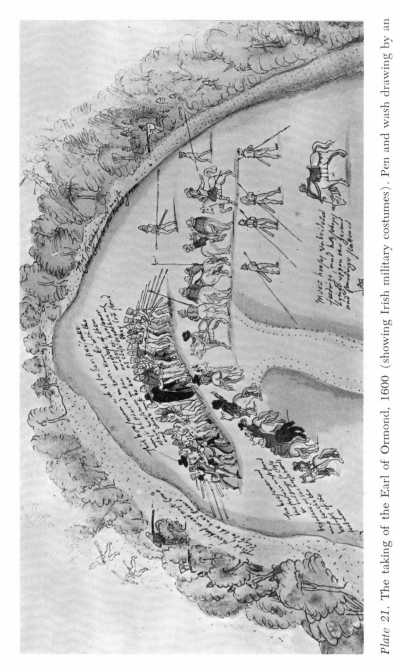

Plate 21. The taking of the Earl of Ormond, 1600 (showing Irish military costumes). Pen and wash drawing by an unknown artist. (Trinity College, Dublin, MS. 1209, no. 13.)

Forasmuch as it is seene, that notwithstanding the good lawes prouided for the restraining of idle people and vagabonds, in default of the reformation thereof by the Iustices of Peace & other Ministers authorized thereto, they are in many partes of the Realme manifestly seene wandering in the common high wayes, to the annoyance of the common people, both in their goods and liues, a multitude of able men, neither impotent nor lame, exacting money continually vpon pretence of seruice in the warres without reliefe, whereas many of them neuer did so serue, and yet such as haue serued, if they were maymed or lamed by seruice, are prouided for in the Countreis, by order of a good Statute made the last Parliament: For reformation whereof, her Maiestie straitly commaundeth all Iustices and Officers, to haue better regard hereto, and to appoynt vpon certaine dayes in the weeke monethly (for some season) watches, and priuie searches in places needfull, and thereby to attach and imprison such idle vagabonds, and to send the lame and maymed into their Countreyes, according to the Statute. And likewise her Maiestie commaundeth the Iustices of assise now in these Lent assises, to conferre with the Iustices in euery County at the place where the assises shalbe kept, and there both to charge them and direct them by some good order, how euery one of them personally shall indeuour themselues in their quarters to see watches to be kept, and priuie searches made for the reformat on hereof, according to the Lawes prouided for this purpose. And furthermore, where it is found that about the Citie of London and in parts neere and about her Maiesties Court, there doe haunt & repaire thither a great multitude of wandring persons, without any iust cause for any seruice to be done to her Maiestie or to her officers or attendants, whereof some are men of Ireland, that haue these late yeeres vnnaturally serued as rebels against her Maiesties forces beyond the Seas, who cannot haue any good meaning towards her Maiestie, as of late hath bin manifestly proued in some already taken, that haue secretly come into the Realme with full purpose, by procurement of the deuil and his ministers her Maiesties enemies, and rebels on the other side the Sea, to endaunger her Maiesties noble person: which kind of persons hauing so serued against her Maiestie, are directly to be taken whatsoeuer they may be found, and proceeded withall as Traytours, And as for the procurers and authors hereof, being knowne to be of sundry conditions, some rebellious subiects fugitiues, some by the order of their Priesthood yeelding dispensation and absolution by shrift to the intended mischiefes, and some others more able by rewarde to hire the offenders, being persons of high degree in the world, the reuenge whereof belongeth to Almightie God, in whose handes her Maiestie hath of long time reposed her selfe, and so intendeth constantly with comforte to continue. But considering the discouerie of these Irish traitours can hardely bee made, where there are also many other like vagrant persons of that Nation that haunt about the Court, by pretence onely of suites, where they haue no iust cause to make any, Therefore her Maiestie for remedy hereof, willeth and commaundeth, that no maner of person borne in the Realme of Ireland, except he be a housholder knowen in some Towne where hee liueth in the obedience of her Maiesties Lawes, or be a meniall seruant with some Nobleman, Gentleman, or other honest housholder, or doe reside, or be in commons in any house of Court or Chauncery, as a student in the Lawes, or a student in any of the vniuersities, or else be sent out of Ireland by her Maiesties Deputy or some Gouernours of the Prouinces there with commendation, or about any seruice or suite recommended, shall remaine in this Realme, but shall without delay repaire into the Realme of Ireland to the places of their naturall habitation, where they ought to liue, vpon paine of imprisonment and punishment as vagabonds.

SOLON HIS FOLLIE,

OR

A POLITIQVE DIS-
COVRSE, TOVCHING THE
Reformation of common-weales conquered, declined or corrupted.

BY RICHARD BEACON GENT. STV-
DENT OF GRAYES INNE, AND SOME-
times her Maiesties Attorney of the province
of Mounster in Irelande.

* *
*

AT OXFORD,
Printed by IOSEPH BARNES, Printer to the Vniversitie,
Anno Domini, 1594.

Plate 23. Title page of Richard Beacon, *Solon His Follie* (Oxford, 1594).

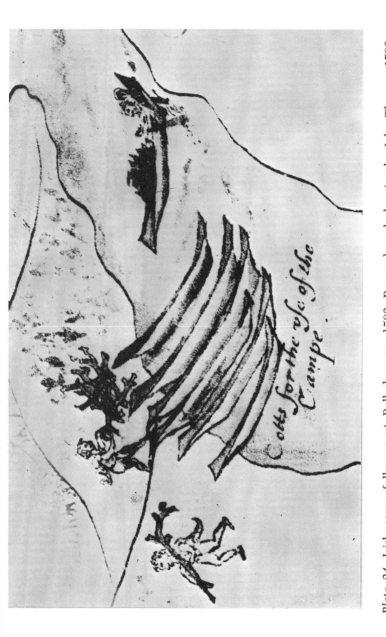

Plate 24. Irish camp followers at Ballyshannon, 1593. Pen and wash drawing by John Thomas, 1593 (detail). (British Museum, Cotton MSS., Augustus, II, 38.)

Cotts for the vse of the Campe.

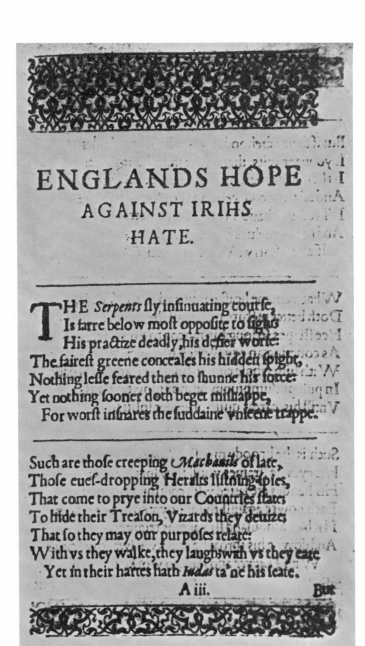

ENGLANDS HOPE
AGAINST IRIHS
HATE.

THE *Serpents* fly infinuating courfe,
Is farre below moft oppofite to fight:
His practize deadly, his defier worfe:
The faireft greene conceales his hidden fpight,
Nothing leffe feared then to fhunne his force:
Yet nothing fooner doth beget mifhappe,
For worft infnares the fuddaine whiefte trappe.

Such are thofe creeping *Machauils* of late,
Thofe euef-dropping Heralts liftning fpies,
That come to prye into our Countries ftate;
To hide their Treafon, Vizards they deuize;
That fo they may our purpofes relate:
With vs they walke, they laugh with vs they eate,
Yet in their hartes hath *Iudas* ta'ne his feate.

A iii.   But

Plate 25. From the copy in the British Museum.

other peoples known to them, speculate on their origins, and attempt to explain their significance. Curiosity in this sphere, as in so many others, tended with Renaissance Englishmen to lead on from random recording to the beginnings of science. Science, of course, in this case, involves a degree of objectivity about one's own society. This is hardest of all for a conquering (or a conquered) people to achieve. Only a measure, sometimes a very small measure indeed, of this was found in the Englishmen who set down their opinions on Tudor Ireland. Most of them wanted to know about Irishmen in order to learn how to turn them into Englishmen. Some of them recorded Irish culture traits in order to have a precise conception of what to destroy, others to have material for satire. At the same time, their attempts at objective observation did produce a fairly coherent picture of what Irish life was like. And in their successive attitudes there were signs of tolerance as well as of hostility—in Campion, in Harington, even in Spenser.

This perhaps has something of a parallel in Mexico and Peru in the second and third generations after the Spanish conquest. The first phase was destruction, as complete and comprehensive as possible, of the native civilization, then a patient attempt to revive on paper its past glories. This is especially true of Peru, where Cieza de León and Pedro Sarmiento de Gamboa, among pure-bred Spaniards, and Garcilaso de la Vega, the Inca, and Pomo de Ayala, among mixed breeds, devoted much of their lives to the understanding of Inca society. Bernardino de Sahagún is an example of the mixed-breed cultural revivalist in Mexico. In Ireland the process of conquest was much more long-drawn-out and so contemporary observations are of great value, although much is to be learned also from seventeenth-century observers looking backward. The English, once they had, to their own satisfaction, established their superiority and were no longer challenged in the areas they had newly conquered, found the natives interesting. This reaction came undoubtedly from the awakening of a genuine intellectual curiosity, though perhaps to a much greater degree from a continuing but now affectionate superiority. The English, it should be noted, were not the creators of the myth of the noble savage, which we may perhaps regard as the reversed wish-fulfillment symbol of European imperialism. In the noble savage, cultivated Europeans first saw primitive man as they wished to see him, not as he was: they then proceeded to wish they, themselves, were like the man they had imagined. But of course this had little or no influence on the behavior of European colonialists in practice. English observers were possibly credulous and hence were misled in the sixteenth century (as they have been in the twentieth) by Irishmen who deliberately misinformed them, but they had a degree of realism in their approach also. The English picture of Ireland and the Irish, if often coarse in the grain, is frequently true enough in the broad outline.

The Irish might be portrayed to English audiences as examples of intellectual backwardness. Thus an English writer in 1550 said that:

If one would carry a globe into Ireland, whose daily turnings would work the same thing in sun, the moon, and the five moveable stars, which is done in heaven every day and every night, which of them would think, in that wild country, the globe to be made without singular cunning? [2]

But the celestial globe at that date might have appeared just such a piece of magic to rural gentry and peasants in England itself.

Of course it was easy for Englishmen to lump all non-Englishmen together, or at least to throw together those who were distinctively different from the English. The English writer George Turberville wrote some verse letters from Russia in 1568 in which he attempted to describe the strange, rather unattractively different, society in which he found himself, and he expressed himself by comparing Ireland and the Irish with Russia and the Russians:

> Wild Irish are as civil as the Russies in their kind,
> Hard choice which is the best of both, each bloody, rude, and
>   blind.[3]

If Turberville's comparison between Russians and Irish is not particularly meaningful, other Englishmen, as they went still further afield, made more effective use of the method. Giles Holmes, for example, reported in 1580 that the Pecheycony people of the mouth of the Ob wore "their hair . . . after the Irish fashion,"[4] though William Towerson, who bartered the gold he was bringing from Guinea with Irish kern in 1556, did not unfortunately make any comparisons between Africans and Irish.[5] Thomas Hariot, however, in 1588 established a pattern of referring North American Indian practices to those of the Irish when he said of the North Carolina Algonkians that they killed fish "with poles made sharp at one end, by shooting them into the fish after the manner as Irishmen cast darts."[6]

In the first forty years of the seventeenth century, as Englishmen penetrated North America, the memories of those who had served in the Irish wars, or who had heard stories from those who had, continued to revive at the sight of North American Indians. Comparisons were most frequently made of costume but they extended also to custom.

In New England in 1602 Gabriel Archer noticed Indians wearing "near their waists" close-fitting leggings of sealskin, "tied fast," he said, "like to Irish 'Dimmie Trouses'" (apparently like abbreviated trews),[7] while Martin Pring at Cape Cod in 1603 noticed an Indian wearing "a bear's skin like an Irish mantle over one shoulder."[8] George Percy, walking in the woods near Jamestown in 1607, remarked, "by chance we espied a pathway like to an Irish pace,"[9] a narrow ride or passage which was the usual road through the boggy or wooded parts of

23

Ireland. John Smith, describing Powhatan's dress in 1608, noted his "fair robe of skins as large as an Irish mantle" [10]— Champlain made the same sort of comparison in 1619.[11] William Strachey, similarly, spoke of "large mantles of divers skins, not much differing from the Irish 'falinges,'" [12] showing he knew the Gaelic word *fallaing* for a mantle. He also called attention to the trews-like leggings which the Virginia Indians wore hunting, "a kind of leather breeches and stockings, all fastened together, made of deerskins, which they tie and wrap about the loins after the fashion of the Turks or Irish trouses." [13] Of their sleeping habits, he says, "some lie stark naked on the ground from six to twenty in a house, as do the Irish." [14] He noted that "the married women wear their hair all of a length, shaven, as the Irish, by a dish," [15] though the comparison here is not borne out by sixteenth-century accounts of Irish hair styles.

The same sort of comparison was made by the authors of *Mourt's Relation,* who noted on March 18, 1621, that the Indians "had, most of them, long hosen up to their groins, closely made, and above their groins to their waist another leather. They were altogether," he said, "like the Irish trouses." [16] William Wood was particularly fond of making comparisons with the Irish, and his 1634 tract is spattered with them. Once again the similarity of Indian leggings with Irish trews is remarked on, though here there may have been some imitation of trousers: "In the wintertime the more aged of them wear leather drawers, in form like Irish trouses, fastened under their girdle with buttons." [17] We are told again, "Many of them wear skins about them in form of an Irish mantle." [18] Less repetitive is what he says of "their unoatmealed broth, made thick with fishes, fowls, and beasts boiled all together, some remaining raw, the rest converted by overmuch seething to a loathed mash, not half so good as Irish 'Boniclapper,'" [19] though boniclabber, as we shall see, was not a stew but a sour-milk drink. Mourning ceremonies also came to his mind when speaking of a dead Indian "over whose grave is for a long time spent many a briny tear, deep groan, and Irish-like howlings." [20]

The summer dwellings of the Irish, while in the booleys, were compared by Thomas Morton in 1632 with those used by the Indians of Massachusetts:

The natives of New England are accustomed to build them houses much like the wild Irish. They gather poles in the woods and put the great end of them in the ground, placing them in form of a circle or circumference and, bending the tops of them in form of an arch, they bind them together with the bark of walnut trees, which is wondrous tough, so that they make the same round on the top for the smoke of their fire to ascend and pass through. These they cover with mats.

Many booley houses were stone built, but others are referred to as being lightly made lodges. It does not seem easy to equate them so directly with the Algonkian long house, nor is it clear that Morton had direct experience of Ireland. He remarks once more on the similarity of the Indian leggings to Irish trews: "When they have their apparel on they look like Irish in their trouses, the stockings join so to their breeches." [21] But after 1640 the use of Irish comparisons with American Indians gradually died along with those who had made them.

Similar use of Irish reference is found elsewhere in the same generation. Thus Richard Jobson compared the Fulby women on the River Gambia in 1620–1621 with the Irish, to the disadvantage of the latter.

I have divers times said there was a great difference between them and the Irish Calios [*cailleacha*, old women], although their manner of lives had great resemblance in following of their Cattle, and as they were out of heart in one ground [i.e., had worn it out by lack of manuring], to remove whole towns together, which but a few years since was the Irish kern's true course of life. But with cleanliness your Irish woman hath no acquaintance.[22]

Describing the burial of a chief, Jobson said:

Just after the same manner as the Irish do use, with a wonderful noise of cries and lamentations, he was laid into the ground; the people, especially the women, running about the house and from place to place with their arms spread after a lunatic fashion, seemed with great sorrow to bewail his departure.[23]

The court of an African chief seemed to him very similar to that of an Irish lord:

There is, without doubt, no people on the earth more naturally affected to the sound of music than these people, which the principal persons do hold as an ornament of their state, so as when we come to see them, their music will seldom be wanting, wherein they have a perfect resemblance to the Irish rhymer, sitting in the same manner as they do upon the ground, somewhat remote from the company. And as they use singing of songs unto their music, the ground and effect whereof is the rehearsal of the ancient stock of the king, exalting his antientry [i.e., the antiquity of his line], and recounting over all the worthy and famous acts [which] by him or them hath been achieved, singing likewise extempore upon any occasion [which] is offered whereby the principal [i.e., the chief] may be pleased.[24]

Jobson in these passages rises at least to the threshold of comparative ethnology, illuminating the characteristics of one pastoral society by those of another.

It is not always easy to know whether the Irish examples arise from direct observation in Ireland or come from conversation, published accounts, or the sight of Irishmen in England. The use of the Irish as the standard of savage or outlandish reference was well established by 1560, as we find Archbishop Parker urging the speedy appointment of resident clergy in parts of the North of England lest the people "should be too much Irish and savage." [25] It was to last until late in the seventeenth century. It may be interesting, too, to note that the reputation of the Irish for wildness extended to Spain, and that Archbishop Oviedo, writing to Philip III about the Earls of Tyrone and Tyrconnell in 1600, found it necessary to say "no como Saluajes sino como prudentíssimos." [26]

The comparison between Irish practices and those of American Indians or Africans was, as the examples above indicate, often purely descriptive, but such comparisons could also have emotional overtones. Gervase Markham, as we shall see, affects to regret that the Irish kern could sink to the practices of the "brutish Indians." When, too, he is delving into a mythical Irish past, he finds the Irish to have been devil-worshipers:

> Even as by histories it still appears
> Th' Americans, until of later years,
> They served no God but Belzibub the great,
> Who in each temple had his sacred grove.[27]

The comparative method, however elementary, was often tied to the historical approach. Edmund Spenser spent much time trying to link Irish customs with earlier barbarian practices, largely seen through the eyes of classical authors but, in some degree, in relation to more recent comparisons with Spain. We may not often find his analogies and etymologies illuminating, though they are so occasionally. William Camden, in successive editions of the *Britannia* from 1586 onward, tried to link Ireland with the classical past and, indeed, to deal as well as he might with the materials at his disposal on the common origins of the peoples of the British Isles. But the historical approach was often more interesting in its method than in its results.

Fynes Moryson [28] proceeded on the opposite track to those who compared American customs with Irish. Less historically minded than Spenser or Camden, he had nonetheless been further afield and had traveled slowly through Germany, the Low Countries, Switzerland, Italy, Denmark, Poland, Austria, and the Near East, not to mention Scotland, before setting foot in Ireland. He had, indeed, sketched out a brief account of his

efore he arrived there for three years of fighting and
ation. His Irish writings are, therefore, colored by his
periences and he is able to make, from time to time,
useful and sometimes penetrating comparisons from his Continental experience, though it may be observed that he had more
familiarity and sympathy with the Continental civilization of
Europe than with the culture of her Atlantic fringes. He is by
far the most experienced observer the Irish of the later Tudor
period had to tolerate. If his comments on the defects of Irish
society as he saw them seem exceptionally harsh, it may be remembered both that he was on the opposing side to the Irish in
the war against Hugh O Neill and that his commentary was
written in a period when the destruction of the remnants of the
old Irish polity was official English policy of which he could
scarcely disapprove in public (though there is no evidence that
he wished to do so). Then, too, he was always somewhat severe
on those not fortunate enough to be born Englishmen and
reared in English cosiness, an environment which he himself
when young could not abide for long. The Venetians and other
Europeans suffered from the same basic defect as the Irish: they
were not English.

Father William Good, who, it appears, wrote the descriptive
text which Camden attributed to "J. Good" when he printed it
in 1607 [29] (it was Englished in 1610 [30]), and which is of more
lasting value than Camden's own careful antiquarian-historical
treatment, was an English Catholic who, after his entry into the
Jesuit order, was posted to Limerick in the 1560's. His approach
is both strongly English and firmly missioner-reformer. The fact
that he never returned to Ireland may suggest that his superiors
did not think him wholly suitable for work in the Irish field, but
his sense of the strangeness of Irish society is vividly conveyed,
and he was a keen though rather limited observer who tried to
set down what he saw and to separate description from comment.

28

Richard Stanyhurst is a rather different type of commentator.[31] As it is a little difficult to distinguish his own views from those of Edmund Campion, it may be as well to mention that Campion came to Ireland in 1569 as a guest of Richard Stanyhurst and his father, James Stanyhurst, Recorder of Dublin and himself a learned man. Out of that visit came Campion's "History of Ireland," completed by the time of his departure in 1571 and including a short commentary on Irish society. It was not published, but Richard Stanyhurst was asked to incorporate what he could of it in the Irish sections, descriptive and historical, which he put together for Raphael Holinshed's *Chronicles* in 1577. He took over some of Campion's sentiments but greatly extended what he wrote about Irish life. We may, however, regard the Campion-Stanyhurst views as virtually a single approach to the Irish problem, originating in the Stanyhurst home in Dublin and being elaborated by father and son after the guest had gone.

Stanyhurst is a remarkable but wayward writer who allows us to look at Ireland from the angle provided by the English Pale. He is a strong protagonist of the Old English and views the Irish encroachments, as he regards them—for example, the re-penetration of the Irish language into the eastern part of the island—with hostility. Nevertheless, he is able to look at the Irish social system with some sympathy and understanding, as well as an appreciable amount of prejudice. His view is much more one from the inside than anything else we have. It was quite natural for him to feel that, however picturesque Irish society was, it must, and ought to, yield to the Anglicizing process. If Campion had shown in the preface to his history [32] a certain sympathy with Irish learning and scholarship which is hardly evident from Stanyhurst's own writing (as Professor R. Dudley Edwards has pointed out [33]), his overall views were molded by the Dubliners, even though he warns his readers not to impute to the Irish "the faults of their ancestors" as set out by the vivid

29

but malicious pen of Gerald of Wales almost four centuries before.

Spenser wrote [34] from long experience of Ireland as well as with a mind well stored with humanistic learning. His employment as Lord Grey's secretary, his residence in County Kildare and his services to the Presidency Council of Munster and, above all, his experiences as a planter in County Cork, enabled him to speak with some authority in both description and analysis. He is the most learned as well as the best writer among the commentators, and the dialogue form of his treatise on Ireland enabled him to suggest more than one way of looking at various Irish problems. He took the trouble to get a certain amount of Irish literature translated for his benefit and to find out something of its techniques from its practitioners. Yet he set his description of Irish life in the context of a program for complete Anglicization and he therefore inevitably adopted an overriding attitude of hostility to the Irish polity, even where parts of his description are objective and some of his comments both friendly and perspicacious. If he misrepresents, and if he does some Irish institutions considerably less than justice, his insights and his gift for language raise *A View of the State of Ireland* (published, it may be remembered, only in 1633) to a high level of accomplishment.

Barnaby Rich was perhaps the sourest of the commentators on the Irish who wrote on the basis of long experience.[35] He was first in Ireland with Essex in 1573 and is last heard of there in 1617. In 1609, when he published *A Short Survey of Ireland,* he professed to be still unwilling to describe the country and the manners of its people fully:

All which, if I should express according to a truth, I might write a more admirable history, and speak of greater wonders than either Sir John Mandeville in his travel or any other that have passed the most uncouth places of the world are able truly to report.[36]

His excuse was here largely a device to allow himself full measure to denounce popery in Ireland, but the following year, in *A New Description of Ireland,* he overcame his reluctance and gave a more general account of the Irish. The result is an odd performance. Rich looks back from a time of almost triumphant plantation in Ireland to the old native society and sees it mostly in jaundiced terms—not least as providing texts against popish dangers—but here and there he describes facets of Irish life vividly and, probably, with some accuracy of detail. By the time of his last book, *The Irish Hubbub* (1617), he has had his say on the Irish and takes most of his time to chastise the Old and New English citizens of Dublin for their real or imagined faults.

Sir John Harington was an engaging writer.[37] A would-be planter in Munster, he came and went in 1587, arousing, though not satisfying, his curiosity about the Irish. On his return in 1599 he made light of the discomforts of military campaigning and took in greedily all he saw in Ireland. His attitude is curiously different from the censorious traveler Moryson: for him Ireland, however primitive conditions might be there, had an abiding charm. He evidently spoke as freely as he thought when he was in Ireland, and his gift for racy expression made him acceptable, it would seem, to Old English and Irish alike. Even when he looked back in 1605 he convinced himself that Ireland was where he most wished to be and where he believed he could temper Anglicization with both humanity and good fellowship. It is not possible to take him too seriously, but it is a relief to find him so susceptible to the attraction of Ireland after reading the stern prescriptions of the more severe reformers.

The half-dozen writers so far mentioned are by no means the only ones, but they provide a good cross section of the observers of Irish society. Among them they give us the majority of the pen pictures of what Irish Ireland was like, as well as the comparisons and the moral, nationalist, and political judgments inside which Englishmen set the Irish society of the time.

The Elizabethans and the Irish

What is most difficult to get and retain in Elizabethan English reactions to Ireland is a sense of proportion. Because the main emphasis is so often on exposing the "evils" of Irish life, the same features tended to be insisted on over and over again, so that it is not always easy to say how large a part they actually played in Irish political or social life. Similarly, too, positive and negative, favorable and unfavorable, comments are sometimes so balanced that one can only report rather than make any precise evaluation, while generalizations made at the time can rarely be seen to be wholly valid and must be taken only as glimpses of a varied reality.

Historical scholarship in Ireland has not yet given us the full and detailed surveys of Irish society which we need before we can obtain a balanced impression of the value of English views on the Irish. The brief descriptions by Gerald A. Hayes-McCoy, David Greene, and others already referred to make it possible to go confidently a little way with the discussion of English views on some topics, and we can consequently see them as correct or incorrect, straight or slanted. We are still at a loss to evaluate many others and can record them only, so that we must still exhibit the Englishman's view of Ireland as a whole on an impressionistic rather than on a scientific basis.

It is clear, however, that Gaelic society in the last century of its autonomous existence presented a number of facets of its ancient heritage, often contradictory, to English observers. The elementary earthiness of Irish peasant life made it appear crude and unpleasant; methods of warfare and the unruly behavior of the Irish military in peace and war made it seem savage. The unfamiliarity of many Irish customs and beliefs revealed Irish society as both outlandish and reprehensible, especially where Irish practices were imperfectly understood. Irish wanderers and wandering customs upset Englishmen, mainly because they seemed to threaten the stability of life in town and village to which they were accustomed. At the same time, the basic simplicity of Irish life had its attractions for some Englishmen. Irish aristocracy had a heroic quality, enhanced by what was known of Irish song and story. The kindness and hospitality of Irishmen could be matched against the less engaging sides of what they had to offer. The appearance of some Irishmen and Irishwomen was as attractive as that of others was repellent. The speed both of Irish feet and of Irish wit could be set against Irish arrogance and Irish anger and the less pleasant Irish tricks.

The English observers throw a great deal of light, though it has its murky patches, on Ireland and the Irish; their remarks also reveal much about themselves. We can emerge after a study of their writings with some insight into the mind of the Elizabethan Englishman in Ireland—curious, surprised, hostile, censorious, nationalistic, reforming, and, paradoxically, at times sympathetic and brutal almost in the same breath.

CHAPTER V

The Irish Polity Characterized

THE distinctness of the Irish kingdoms, or lordships, as it is probably less confusing to call them, is well brought out by a writer who told Henry VIII early in his reign:

There be more than sixty countries . . . inhabited with the King's Irish enemies, . . . where reigneth more than sixty chief captains, whereof some calleth themselves kings, some king's peers, in their language . . . and every of the said captains makes war and peace for himself, and holds by [the] sword, and hath imperial jurisdiction within his "room" and obeys no other person.[1]

Though it was recognized that the O Neills in Ulster, for example, had made clients of the rulers of the other lordships of Ulster, there is not, I think, any clear admission in English sources that the O Neills were traditionally provincial kings of Ulster, a dignity which their acceptance of an earldom from the Tudors did not override. Indeed, whether or not they made agreements in accordance with the policy of surrender and regrant, the Irish lords proved, down to 1603, unwilling to accept English monarchical authority as the ultimate limitation on their power. Fynes Moryson regarded them as autocratic and tyrannical—"the lords, or rather chiefs of countries, . . . being absolute tyrants over their people, themselves eating upon them and

making them feed their kern, or footmen, and their horsemen" [2]
—and gave an impression of the country people living under the
lords like slaves.

Laying down a didactic definition of the Irish ruler, Sir William Gerrard, Lord Chancellor of Ireland, in 1578 said:

> The Irish is known by name, speech, habit, feeding, order, rule and
> conversation. He accounteth himself chief in his own country and
> (whatsoever he say or profess) liketh of no superior. He mortally
> hateth the English. By will he governeth those under him, supplying
> his and their wants by preying and spoiling of other countries adjoin-
> ing. These live as the Irish lived in all respects before the Conquest. [3]

A full and in many ways credible description of Irish government in detail is given by Edward Tremayne, clerk of the Irish
Privy Council, in 1573. It demonstrates on the one side considerable knowledge of Irish practices, and on the other appreciable
misconceptions of the extent to which Irish rulers (most of
them at least) were bound by a network of custom and traditional law which remained for the most part invisible to the
English observer. He says:

> The Irish government, as I at the least have conceived, is that one
> great lord possesseth and ruleth a Country, sometimes as big as an
> English shire, sometimes more, sometimes less, as it happeneth. He
> attaineth unto it rather by choice and election than succession. In
> which election they observe to choose him of the kindred (which
> they call "septe") of such as have been used to rule them. Such are
> Oneale, Odonell, Oreley, Ocarroll and such others. And for the most
> part he that hath showed himself most mischievous in murdering,
> spoiling, and burning doth soonest attain to the government, first to
> be "thaniste" (which is as it were heir in succession), and afterward
> to be the ruler when the lord in possession dieth. When this great
> lord is thus in possession of his Country, he is followed of all the
> warlike people of the same, viz., horsemen, galloglasses, and kern,
> and with these multitudes he useth the inferior people at his will and
> pleasure. He eateth and spendeth upon them with man, horse, and

35

dog. He useth man, wife, or children according to his own list, without any means to be withstanded or again-said, not only as an absolute king but as a tyrant or a lord over bondsmen. For deciding of causes in controversies he hath a judge of his own constitution and useth the law called the Brehon Law, nothing agreeing with the laws of England. If any of his people commit an offense, he is punished or pardoned as pleaseth the lord. If any of his people receive wrong or any offense be done against his Country, this great lord useth the revenge according to his own will, without making any stay for commission for the Queen or her governor. So as, in short terms, a man may say the Irish rule is such a government as the mightiest do what they list against the inferiors.[4]

Some English officials, indeed, found it difficult to recognize the existence of any order in the Irish polity. Connacht, to Sir Edward Fitton in 1573, was "not worthy to be called a commonwealth." [5] He maintained that there was "not justice amongst the people, but force beareth all the sway. The poor sort destroyed, the greatest live miserably and in continual dissension, murdering and spoiling without ceasing." Nor could Sir Richard Bingham find more coherence in 1596: "The wastes there [are] no other than a Tartarian waste, which is, if one part be waste, another be inhabited, the manner of the people being as it is to remove with their cattle from place to place." [6]

Yet Captain Nicholas Dawtrey, an old Irish hand who is seen by some as an original for Falstaff, linked Irish intransigence with old custom and based political judgments on this analysis in his petition to the Queen in June, 1594, at a time when Ireland was still thought fairly peaceful:

For although that the said Irish Septs have had at your Majesty's hands all grace, favor, and pardon from time to time of their faults, with many rewards and gifts, rather to win them than for their deserts, yet as they still prove, of what condition or state soever they be, according to the old proverb, which is, that an ape will be an ape, though he were clad in cloth of gold. The civilest of all these Irish races, be he ever so small in ability or command, can hardly forgo their tyrannous customs, that is, that they will not have or suffer this one maxim of justice to be distinguished amongst them, which is, *Meum* and *tuum*.

For they will have all that their sword can command and depart [i.e., part] with nothing that the same sword can keep. And [they] do also hold their pedigrees and genealogies even to prove their descents directly or indirectly to be descended from the ancient barbarous kings of that realm, that were before the English conquest. Delighting in all their Irish assemblies by speech of the people, songs, rhymes, and "daynes [*dáin*, poems]" to be called "Mackire [*Mac ríogh* or *Mac an ríogh*]" and "Ennion Mackire [*Inghean ríogh* or *Inghean an ríogh*]," which is to say the king's son and the king's daughter; and then to have services done them by the name of "Kish Mackire [*cíos ríogh*, king's tribute; perhaps *cíos mhac an ríogh*, king's son's services]," which is as much as to say the king's rents or services. So long as these titles and services is suffered and used without punishment or correction for the same, it is impossible but that their hearts should be so puffed up with vainglory as that they cannot endure obedience where they owe it in troth longer than the sword hangeth over their heads or that your Majesty set your foot on their necks.[7]

With approaches such as these it was sometimes hard for Englishmen to get their bearings. Spenser said that the tenants of an Irish lord had no security of tenure and were therefore always at his mercy,[8] while Moryson maintained that "they distribute their lands among their tenants, to be tilled only for one, two, or three years." [9] But he and other writers tended to assume that all the lands in the Irish territories were at the disposal of the lord, while in fact only his family lands and those belonging to his office, and not the greater part in the possession of the freemen, were so available. It may be that there is something in Moryson's further statement that "these lords, challenging all their tenants' goods, think scorn to have any cows or cattle of their own," but it is not at all likely to be true of more than certain individual lordships. Certainly annual tenures were common enough. Sir Henry Sidney in 1576, speaking of Ulster affairs, said, "At May Day, commonly, the Irish captains and lords use to bargain and compound with their tenants." [10] But this, in a society where little fixed capital was locked up in the land, did not necessarily strengthen the lord's authority; it might indeed enable the tenants to move away to the care of a less demanding landlord. There was, however, in a society in a state of flux, as in some sense the Gaelic kingdoms had been since the Norman invasion and in which they remained in Elizabethan times, an increase in the powers of the lord.[11] On the one hand the legal system reached back into antiquity to tie almost every economic, social, and political action down to traditional rules, and on the other there was the actual practice of sometimes despotically inclined Irish rulers. In the present state of historical knowledge it is impossible to steer a clear passage between the two and to know what was typical and what was exceptional. The effective—as distinct from the legal—status of the freeman remains obscure.

The difficulty with English accounts of how free the Irish lord was in his dealings with his followers is that it is often impossible to know how far the remarks spring from knowledge of the facts or from ignorance of Irish law and social custom. The common people, it is clear, were of little account in this aristocratic society. And yet Irish cohesion and pride struck the English, not usually in a favorable manner. Moryson says, "The Irish are by nature very factious, all of a sept or name living together, and cleaving close one to another in all quarrels and actions whatsoever, in which kind they suffer great men to eat upon them, and take whatever they have, proverbially saying Defend me and spend me." [12] On their pride he maintains that the lords and gentlemen under them are "by nature proud and disdainful of reproach." [13] Stanyhurst, as one of the Old English, had been at the receiving end of their scorn: "The Irishman standeth so much upon his gentility that he termeth anyone of the English sept and planted in Ireland 'Bobdeagh Galteagh' [*bodach galldacht*], that is, English churl; but if he be an Englishman born, then he nameth him 'Bobdeagh Saxonnegh' [*bodach saxanach*], that is, a Saxon churl: so that both are churls and he the only gentleman." [14] Father Good emphasized their conservatism, "stiffly settled in observing of the old rites of their country," and complained of "a certain peevish and obstinate love they bear unto their own country fashions." [15] Andrew Boorde, indeed, found already in the 1540's that a proud resentment was one of the more prominent Irish characteristics. His Irishman says:

> My anger and my hastiness doth hurt me full sore:
> I cannot leave it, it 'creaseth more and more;
> And although I be poor I have an angry heart.[16]

The aristocratic nucleus of Irish society produced large households of men who disdained any occupation except fighting and so conduced to idleness. Moryson says, "The Irish in general . . . being slothful and given to nothing more than base idleness, . . . the basest of them will be reputed gentlemen and swordmen, for so are they termed who profess to live by their swords." He shrewdly drew an analogy with the great houses of late medieval and early Tudor England, which were often centers for thieving and plundering as a result of idle servingmen swarming in them, especially in the northern parts of the country, and as was now also the case in Ireland, "where the multitude of loose followers hath of old been prone to fight their lords' quarrels." [17]

By the sixteenth century the core of Irish local autonomy was the existence of an elaborate military system of which we have various descriptions. The highest grade in it was the "horseman, which is the chiefest next the lord and captain," Stanyhurst tells us.[18] "Their horsemen are all gentlemen (I mean of great septs

ow base soever otherwise)," says Moryson.[19] "These
vhen they have no stay of their own [i.e., are not re-
ny particular lord], gad and range from house to
rrant knights of the Round Table, and they never
dismount until they ride into the hall and as far as the table":
this is from Stanyhurst [20] also, not, as might be thought, from
Spenser. Next in order came the galloglasses, heavily armed
footmen, "men . . . commonly wayward rather by profession
than by nature, grim of countenance, tall of stature, big of limb,
burly of body, well and strongly timbered, chiefly feeding on
beef, pork, and butter," as Stanyhurst described them graphically.[21] Edward Tremayne considered them much more estima-
ble socially than other Irish soldiers, "the galloglasses for the
most part being gentlemen, and in time of peace using to live
honestly upon their lands." [22]

An anonymous account of 1588 gives us a somewhat more
technical version. The galloglasses are:

Picked and select men of great and mighty bodies and cruel without
compassion. . . . They are armed with a shirt of mail, a skull, and
a skean. The weapon which they most use is a battle-ax or halberd,
six foot long, the blade whereof is somewhat like a shoemaker's knife,
but broader and longer without pike [i.e., spike], the stroke whereof
is deadly where it lighteth.[23]

They have a man as harness bearer and a boy to carry provi-
sions. "He [the galloglass] is called a spear, of his weapon or ax
so termed, eighty of which spears make a battle of galloglass."
Below them again, was the kern, a foot soldier, lightly armed
with "a skean, a target of wood, a bow and sheaf, or else three
darts, which they cast with wonderful facility." The latter are
"more noisome, especially to the horse, than deadly," according
to the same account. Stanyhurst, writing in the 1570's, says the
kern sometimes carried a firearm.[24] In O Neill's war, at the end
of the reign, the kern was armed, so far as possible, as Moryson

shows, with the harquebus, a moderately portable gun, becoming, on occasion, an effective musketeer.[25]

Spenser was particularly hostile to the lowest grades of foot soldiers [26]—"young wags called Daltins [*dailtín*, fosterling, brat], . . . lackeys . . . serviceable to the grooms or horseboys, who are a degree above the Daltins," as Stanyhurst characterizes them [27]—while Spenser talks also of "the fry of these rakehelly horseboys, growing up in knavery and villainy," who provide recruits for the kern, since, "having been once brought up an idle horseboy, he will never after fall to labor." The horsemen, the anonymous account tells us, take them into the fight to feed and dress the horses and also to throw darts.[28] Spenser is also most bitter in his denunciation of the Irish soldier in general: "From the time that they enter into that course," he says, "they do use all the beastly behavior that may be to oppress all men: . . . they steal, they are cruel and bloody, full of revenge, and delighting in deadly execution; licentious swearers and blasphemers, common ravishers of women and murderers of children." [29] Nevertheless he gives them high marks as combatants: "Yet sure they are very valiant and hardy, for the most part great endurers of cold, labor, hunger, and all hardness, very active and strong of hand, very swift of foot, very vigilant and circumspect in their enterprises, very present in perils, very great scorners of death." The Irish soldier, indeed, he continues, "even in that rude kind of service . . . beareth himself very courageously."

But Irish warfare was not, in general, one of set battles. Irish soldiers were adapted to hit-and-run tactics. Moryson comments: "Because they are only trained to skirmish upon bogs and difficult passes or passages of woods, and not to stand or fight in a firm body upon the plains, they think it no shame to fly or run off from fighting, as they advantage." [30] "In war," says Father Good, "they use the bagpipe instead of a trumpet . . . and in joining battle they cry as loud as possible they can 'Pharroh' [apparently *Faire! Faire!* Watch out! Beware!]" [31] They were also very susceptible to the praise or blame of the poets; and "so affected to vainglory," says Moryson, "as they nothing so much feared the Lord Deputy's anger as the least song or ballad these rascals might make against them." [32] The influence of the bards was probably greatest on the soldiery; it was considerable right through Irish society.

Honor and praise were eagerly sought after by Irish lords: "To this end," as Stanyhurst put it, "they esteem their poets, who write Irish learnedly and pen their sonnets heroical, for the which they are bountifully rewarded; if not they send out libels in dispraise, whereof the lords and gentlemen stand in great awe." [33] Spenser had had some Irish writings translated to him and, as a poet, took a professional interest in their form and content. He, too, recorded the influence the poets had at the lord's court through their eulogies and satires: "Their verses are taken up with a general applause and usually sung at all feasts and meetings by certain other persons whose proper function that is, which also receive for the same great rewards, and reputation besides." [34] The singing was done, usually, to the harp. Father Good says, "Delighted they are above measure in music, but especially in the harp with wire strings, which they warble upon with their nimble fingers most melodiously." [35] This lay order of poets had existed by the sixteenth century, Professor David Greene tells us, for some four hundred years as a well-defined hereditary body, using a standard language taught, with its accompanying metrical usages, in a seven-year course of study. [36] An Englishman, Smyth by name, early in Queen Elizabeth's reign, wrote down some notes on the learned classes which are of considerable interest. [37] He was mainly concerned to see in them a bad influence which the English should eliminate. He speaks of the " 'Shankee' [*seanchaidhe*, storyteller or genealogist], which is to say in English, the 'petigrer' [i.e., pedigree-er]. They have also great plenty of cattle. . . . They make the ignorant men of the country to believe that they be descended of Alexander the Great, or of Darius, or of Caesar, or of some other notable prince." The heroic tales had, Smyth says, a deplorable effect, making "the ignorant people to run mad, and careth not what they do." Stanyhurst is perhaps going to the opposite extreme of sophistication when he tells us that "one office in the house of noblemen is a taleteller, who bringeth his lord asleep with tales vain and frivolous, whereunto the number give sooth and credit." [38] Of greater account, Smyth says, were the " 'Fillis' [*filidh*], which is to say in English, a poet. These men have great store of cattle and use all the trades of the others with an addition of prophecy," since originally they were seers as well as poets. Smyth thought their influence so great as to lead him to believe they were "maintainers of witches." A somewhat lower grade of poet, specializing in panegyric, was, he tells us, "the 'Aeosdan' [*aos dána*], which is to say in English, the bards or the rhyming septs," who are, he thinks, particularly dangerous, as they incite men to violence by reference to their ancestors' feats and by comparison with famous fighting characters of the past. In particular, if they could incite Irishmen to go out on robbing forays, they would get a share of the spoil as their reward.[39] This kind of incitement, at rather an exalted level, we can find in the poem Tadhg Dall Ó Huiginn wrote for Conn O Donnell (d. 1583):

It is easy for thee to win triumphs. The Sons of *Mil* are eager for war; it needs few forays, thou man of the Inny, to stir up Banbha.

A house takes fire from the one beside it; if thy intention of battle be heard, from thy head of wavy tresses the rest will take it; it is a ready desire that is ignited.

Even as the spreading of a flame, throughout the Plain of *Cobhthach* every territory will have its own reaver, from thy raids upon the foreign soldiery.[40]

But the humbler raiders too might have their songs, and these were not always so optimistic. In one of them a man says:

You and I will go to Finegall,
You and I will eat such meats as we find there.
You and I will steal such beef as we shall find fat.
I shall be hanged and you shall be hanged. What shall our children do?
When teeth do grow unto themselves as their fathers did before? [41]

The poets made their living mainly from the gifts of the lords to whom they made verses, but, under English pressure, the chances of obtaining a living in the traditional way were declining. Douglas Hyde translates one poem which was the reaction of a Wicklow poet, Angus O Daly, to seeing the head of his lord impaled on the walls of Dublin:

O body which I see without a head,
It is the sight of thee which has withered up my strength.
Divided and impaled in Ath-cliath,
The learned of Banba will feel its loss.
Who will relieve the wants of the poor?
Who will bestow cattle on the learned?
O body, since thou art without a head,
It is not life which we care to choose after thee.[42]

The bards were so influential amongst the Irish that their services were even called on by the English. Sir John Perrot, making his apologia to Queen Elizabeth after his conviction (on rather dubious grounds) for treason, declared, "I have given money to rhymers to set forth her Majesty's most worthy praises, as by Master Treasurer of the War's accounts will appear." [43] Since he had harried the bards in Munster, he may not always have got precisely the kind of verses he paid for. And Florence Mac-Carthy Mor, an Irish lord who offered his services in 1602 to Sir Robert Cecil to quell the last embers of the Munster rising, proposed to send for messengers, "the best learned and spoken in that language, of special trust, credit, and authority, . . . to persuade that country gentlemen." [44] These were "rhymers, some [of whom] may be trusted only by those gentlemen whose followers they are by line of descent and of whom depends their living." It is as well here to recall what a member of the O Daly family of poets once wrote to an Earl of Desmond: "In poetry for the English we promise that the Gael shall be banished from Ireland; in poetry for the Gaels we promise that the English shall be routed beyond the sea." [45]

The other main element in the learned class was the brehon (*breitheamh*, jurist), "liable to certain families," says Stanyhurst,[46] who "before they will give judgment," Smyth adds, "they will have pawns of both the parties, the which is called in Irish 'Ulieg' [*oile dhéag*, a twelfth, in the special sense of the brehon's fee], and then they will give judgment according to their discretions." [47] "The brehon sitteth on a bank" (to return to Stanyhurst), "the lords and gentlemen at variance round him, and then they proceed." "They will take upon them to judge matters and redress causes as well of inheritance as of other matters, although they are ignorant," Smyth maintains. It was strongly held that Irish law had never been committed to paper (the ancient law tracts and commentaries not being known either to Spenser or Moryson). Spenser defines the Brehon Law as "a certain rule of right, unwritten, but delivered by tradition from one to another, in which oftentimes there appeareth great show of equity in determining the right between party and party, but in many things repugning quite both to God's law and man's." [48] He took, as did most English writers, a strong line against monetary composition in criminal cases, particularly capital ones, saying that "in the case of murder, the Brehon . . . will compound between the murderer and the friends of the party murdered, which prosecute the action, that the malefactor shall give unto them, or to the child or wife of him that is slain, a recompense which they call an 'Iriach' [*éiric*, compensation], by which vile law many murders are amongst them made up and smothered." We learn a little about procedure. "They will have pawns of both the parties," says Smyth, "and then will they give judgment according to their own discretion" [49]; Moryson adding, "Before these judges no probable or certain arguments were available to condemn the accused, but only manifest apprehensions in the fact." [50] The brehons were accused of being greedy, Moryson saying, "They did extort unreasonable rewards for their judgment, as the eleventh part of every particular thing brought in question before them," being especially severe on the parties in matrimonial cases, where they demanded many cows, "which are the Irish rewards and bribes." Spenser thought they also worked in their lord's interest, adjudging "for the most part a better share unto his lord, that is the lord of the soil or the head of that sept, and also unto himself for his judgment a greater portion than unto the plaintiffs or parties grieved." [51] Smyth stressed the high status which the brehons held: "These men be neuters [i.e., noncombatants], and the Irishmen will not prey [on] them. They have great plenty of cattle." He also accused them of harboring "many vagabonds and idle persons" and of maintaining rebels against the royal authority.[52]

Cattle raiding was a universal sport; it was a means by which the young man made a test of his manhood; it was not, in many circumstances, regarded as a crime. English commentators regarded it as a symptom of a thievish and plundering society. Stanyhurst is less censorious than many, being able to look at it partly from an Irish point of view: "To rob and spoil their enemies they deem it none offense, nor seek any means to recover their loss, but . . . watch them the like turn." [53] But spoiling associates was an offense: "If neighbors and friends send their purveyors to purloin one another, such actions are judged by the brehons aforesaid." Father Good, looking at this scene through the cleric's eyes (after his Irish experience he went to be a Jesuit missionary in Sweden and Poland), was dismayed:

They account it no shame or infamy to commit robberies, which they practice everywhere with exceeding cruelty. When they go to rob, they pour out their prayers to God "that they may meet with a booty," and they suppose that a cheat or booty is sent unto them from God as His gift; neither are they persuaded that either violence or rapine or manslaughter displeaseth God, for in no wise would He present unto them this opportunity if it were sin.[54]

We thus have the brehons frequently ignoring the cattle raid (*creach*) and the poets exciting men to make such raids and celebrating them when completed successfully. Smyth gives a Rake's-Progress-like account of the wild young man and his bards. Inspired by the poets' celebrations of past raids,

he will gather a rabble of rakehells to him, and he must also get a prophet [the *fili*, in his prophetic guise], who shall tell him how he shall speed, as he thinks. Then will he get him lurking to the side of a wood and there he keepeth himself close until morning; and when it is daylight they will go to the poor villages, . . . burning the houses and corn and ransacking of the poor cottages. They will drive all the kine and plow horses, with all other cattle, and drive them away, . . . and when he is in a safe place they will fall to the division of the spoil, according to the discretion of the captains.[55]

Next, there must be a poem in celebration, and Smyth's story of its performance is, Professor Greene says, of great value, since "nowhere in Irish is there an account of the recital of a poem." [56] The description is:

Now comes the rhymer that made the rhyme, with his "rakry" [*reacaire*, reciter]. The "rakry" is he that shall utter the rhyme; and the rhymer himself sits by with the captain very proudly. He brings with him also his harper, who plays all the while that the "rakry" sings the rhyme. Also he has his bard, which is a kind of foolish fellow [evidently an apprentice], who must also have a horse given him; the harper must have a new saffron shirt and a mantle and a hackney [i.e., a riding horse]; and the "rakry" must have twenty or

47

thirty kine and the rhymer himself horse and harness, with a nag to ride on, a silver goblet, and a pair of beads of coral, with buttons of silver—and this with more they look for to have.[57]

There were other learned men, too, who put their learning to practical use. Indeed, Stanyhurst praises the application of Irish students to Latin learning. "Without either precepts or observations of congruity," he says, "they speak Latin like a vulgar language, learned in their common schools of leechcraft and law, whereat they begin [as] children and hold on sixteen or twenty years, conning by rote the aphorisms of Hippocrates [58] and the civil institutes,[59] with a few other parings of those faculties." The conditions under which learning took place were not good. "In their schools," he tells us, "they grovel upon couches of straw, their books at their noses, themselves flat prostrate, and so they chant out with a loud voice their lessons by piecemeal, repeating two or three words thirty or forty times together." [60] The physicians, we are told, mostly used texts in Irish, drawn from those of the medieval revival of classical medicine, but they are likely also to have used a few printed texts in Latin, as well as traditional compilations of remedies handed down in the family of their teachers.[61] It seems, indeed, that there was much learning by rote. There is no good description of the Irish physician at his work in the narratives, so that we have no clear impression of how he appeared to the English. Besides the doctors there were "wise women" to whom recourse was had in certain illnesses, Moryson mentioning that those who are sick of the fever called the Irish ague "do not use the help of the physician, but give themselves to the keeping of Irishwomen, who starve the ague, giving the sick man no meat, who takes nothing but milk and some vulgarly known remedies at their hand." [62] Thomas Smyth, an apothecary who came over to serve the army about 1556 and later settled down to medical practice in Dublin, complained in 1571 that he could not sell his "drugs and apothecary wares" in Dublin, since the greater part of the people of

Irish birth preferred the ministrations of their own "leeches and physicians." [63] Later, with the help of a government pension and the flowing in of a new tide of soldiers, he prospered (he may, incidentally, be the Smyth who wrote about the bards and brehons).

Though Father Good, as an agent of the Catholic Counter Reformation in Ireland, could find nothing to say for the Irish parish clergy, whose life he described as a filthy one, and was as severe as missioners usually are on the lewd ways of the people at large, he also spoke of the capacity of Irishmen for the religious life. "Do any of them betake themselves to religion," he says, "a wonder it is to see how they mortify and keep their bodies under with a devout kind of austerity, watching, praying, and making themselves lean with much fasting." He concludes "that it is no marvel which is written of their monks in the age aforegoing." [64] Moreover, men of holy life were spared from violence. Stanyhurst tells us, "They honor and reverence friars and pilgrims, by suffering them to pass quietly and by sparing their mansions, whatsoever outrage they show to the country." [65]

The lords, the young men of noble birth, the soldiers, the learned men—brehons, bards, and physicians—the lax priests, the ascetic friars and devout pilgrims (as also the carefully fasting women), emerge with varying degrees of clarity from these characterizations. There is little anywhere about the common people, workers by hand at crafts or on farms, who were held in contempt and beneath notice, apart from occasional mention in English writings of their hard lot. A little, but only a little, more light is thrown on them when we inquire how the Irish were taxed.

The English observers saw little in the way of monetary taxation, apart from the "black rents" which some of the Irish lords, settled near English areas, levied in return for imposing some degree of restraint on the raiding habits of their followers. Most of the levies on their own people were made in kind. Moryson tells us that when the Irish lords and their followers went out "coshering [*cóisireacht,* feasting], they go (as it were) on progress, to live upon their tenants, till they have consumed all the victuals that the poor men have or can get." [66] But these were occasions for feasting and pleasure, in spite of the pain of paying for the entertainment, which fell upon the agriculturists. "Their noblemen, and noblemen's tenants," says Stanyhurst, "now and then make a set feast, which they call coshering, whereto flock all their retainers, whom they name followers, their rhymers, their bards, their harpers that feed them with music: and when the harper twangeth or singeth a song all the company must be whist [i.e., be quiet] or else he chafeth like a cutpurse, by reason his harmony is not had in better price." [67]

Barnaby Rich has left us a slightly more specific description of coshering:

Good company, both of men and women, being drawn together a-feasting, to entertain the time between meals they have their "Rithmers" and their Harpers, the one to sing, and the other to play. . . . The manner of their sitting in this great feasting is this: stools nor tables they have none, but, a good bundle of straw strewed about the floor, they set themselves down one by another. Another burden of straw, being shaken over their legs, doth serve them to set on their dishes. Perhaps, if it be in the time of summer, . . . in the stead of straw they use green rushes. . . . This is both table and tablecloth, whereon they use to place their dishes. Victual they shall have plenty—beef, mutton, pork, hens, rabbits, and all together served in a great wooden platter. Aqua vitae they must have in good store, or else it is not worthy to be called a feast. . . . And commonly the Irish custom is that when they are served with flesh, they have no bread with their meat, but if their store be such that they have bread, their finest manchets are ordinarily oaten-cakes.[68]

The "cuddy" (*cuid oidhche,* a night's entertainment) was another form of institutionalized hospitality. Sir Warham St. Leger describes it in 1589 as "a night supper [which] doth warrant the

lord, with such company that pleaseth him, to come to th
charged therewith, and to take meat and drink for him a
company for the space of four meals at four times in the yea
It is worth noting here how precise and uncasual this sys
of lordly progress was. We may take it that, unless the individual lord was successfully tyrannical or war drove him to emergency dealings with his tenants, many other Irish impositions
were also much more closely defined by Irish law and practice
than English writers, who saw in them solely arbitrary exactions,
realized—which is not to say, of course, that they could not be
burdensome as well as definite.

Moryson says that the Irish lords regarded all the cows and
other property of their people as their own, to be retaken at
their pleasure.[70] Irish social custom was far from being so simple as this, but it was certainly true that exceptional levies might
be taken from the peasantry either in kind or in money. The
lords, Moryson says, do not take any rent from them for their
lands,

> but at pleasure impose money upon them [their people] upon all
> occasions of spending, as journeys to Dublin or into England, paying
> their debts, entertaining of the Lord Deputy or judges, and like oc-
> casions, sometimes true, sometimes feigned, taking a great or small
> portion of their goods according to the quality of the cause. And
> these exactions they do well call cuttings, wherewith they do not
> only cut but devour the people.[71]

He also made the point that such protection as some Irish freemen had against their lords was overridden in the exigencies of
the struggle, under O Neill's leadership, at the end of the period.

Less occasional and less casual was taxation for military pur-
poses. Irish soldiers were paid partly in land they occupied,
partly by levies in kind from the territory on which they were
quartered. Bonaght [*buannacht bhona*] was the basic levy "of
victuals and money of their finding," as John Dymmok, writing
in 1600, has it, on top of which could be charged an additional

definite charge, "Bonaght beg [*buannacht bheag*], a proportion of money, ratably charged upon every plowland," while the troops imposed might also levy a "soren [*sorthan*], . . . a kind of allowance over and above the bonaght, . . . by way of spending money." [72] If the whole *buannacht* was uncertain, that is, was free quarter at discretion, it was known as *buannacht bairr*. This, in turn, appears to be equated with coyne (*coinnmheadh*), which was "as much as to say a placing of men and boys upon the country," says a description of Ireland in 1588, "used by a prerogative of the Brehon Law, whereby they are permitted to take meat, drink, aqua vitae, and money of their hosts without pay-making therefrom. And besides rob them when they have done. As many as keep 'idlemen' [kerns out of active employment, but on the strength] take it outrageously where they come. And by the custom of the country it was lawful to place themselves upon whom they would." [73] With "coyne" was always associated "livery," though the latter word is Norman-French, not Irish, in origin. To quote Dymmok again:

Livery is horsemeat for the horses of those which take coyne or otherwise send them to the poor tenants to be fed. The tenants must find the horses and boys and give them as much corn and sheaf oats as they will have and, for want of oats, wheat and barley. If there be four or five boys to a horse (as sometimes there be), the poor tenants must be contented therewith and yet reward the boys with money.[74]

If the host wished to get rid of the men for a time, he had to buy them off with " 'foy' [possibly *fiach*, a fine], which is where their idlemen require meat out of mealtime or where they take money for their coyne of the host to go a-begging to their neighbors. It is as much as to say a benevolence [a 'free gift' that was not always free]." We may gather that coyne and livery was exacted with least rule or order on the territories of those Old English lords who had adopted it (for example, the

Earls of Desmond) and that there was, normally, in Irish law some limit to the burdens imposed, even though they might be still very heavy. Only this system of billeting soldiers had preserved the Irish lordships from conquest: English observers would suggest that they had almost ruined the peasant in the process, but this may be an exaggeration.

At war, Ireland appears as a land of forays and ambushes, military display, oppression, and destruction. At peace, the lords lived an easy life, hunting, training and exercising their horses, entertaining and feasting, collecting their dues; the peasantry could relax somewhat from the pressures of war, the wanderers take to the roads more freely; the kerns, turned "idlemen," might still disturb the peace by cattle-thieving and by violence to travelers on the roads and trackways through the woods.

Spenser tells us how the Irish people in summer moved en masse to their upland pastures "to live . . . in booleys [*buailte*], pasturing upon the mountain and waste wild places and removing still to fresh land as they have depastured the former days, . . . driving their cattle continually with them and feeding only on their milk and white meats [milk products]." [75] This practice was quite strange to most Englishmen, but Spenser knew it was also used in Scotland (as well as amongst the Scythians of old). He had some notion of its economic importance in the Irish economy, it being desirable, "in this country of Ireland, where there are great mountains and waste deserts full of grass, that the same should be eaten down and nourish many thousand of cattle." He was hostile to it for both social and political reasons:

But by this custom of booleying there grow in the meantime many great enormities unto that commonwealth. For first, if there be any outlaws or loose people, as they are never without some which live upon stealths and spoils, they are ever more succored and find relief only in these booleys, being upon the waste places, where else they should be driven shortly to starve or to come down to the towns to seek relief, where by one means or another they would soon be caught. Besides, such stealths of cattle as they make they bring commonly to these booleys, where they are received readily and the thief harbored from danger of law or such officers as might light upon him. Moreover, the people that live thus in these booleys grow thereby the more barbarous and live more licentiously than they could in towns, . . . for there they think themselves half exempted from law and obedience and, having once tasted freedom, do, like a steer that hath been long out of his yoke, grudge and repine ever after to come under rule again.

We thus see in Spenser the overlaying of the acute observer by the Anglicizing official.

The masterless men who straggled up and down the country were peculiarly obnoxious to Englishmen. Spenser wrote with special intensity about the professional gamblers, "carrowes [cearrbhaigh]," which are

a kind of people that wander up and down gentlemen's houses, living only upon cards and dice, the which, though they have little or nothing of their own, yet will they play for much money, which if they win they waste most lightly, and if they lose they pay as slenderly, but make recompense with one stealth or another. Whose only hurt is not that they themselves are idle losels, but that through gaming they draw others to like lewdness and idleness.[76]

Moryson is also censorious but says, amusingly,

Professed gamesters go about carrying cards and dice with them, and they will not only play for all the money and clothes they have, but even for the members of their body at a rate of money, suffering themselves to be tied by those members and to be led about till they can free them by paying the rate of money.[77]

"And to these may be added," Spenser goes on,

another sort of like loose fellows, which do pass up and down amongst gentlemen by the name of jesters [abhlóiri], but are indeed notable rogues and partakers not only of many stealths by setting forth other men's goods to be stolen, but also privy to many traitorous practices and common carriers of news, with desire whereof you would wonder how much the Irish are fed, for they use commonly to send up and down to know news and if any meet another his second word is, "What news?" [78]

Moryson and Spenser agreed [79] that these wanderers should be wiped out, the former saying, "Could a provost-marshal be better employed than in hanging up such rascals and like vagabond persons?"

We might think that comments like these were casual social criticisms, not serious political pronouncements on which solemn engagements between the Dublin government and Irish or Old English lords might be based. Yet the agreement which the fifteenth Earl of Desmond was forced to make in 1564 to get rid of certain Irish institutions in the lands he owned or influenced makes it possible to think that perhaps English administrators found it difficult, as Englishmen have been known to do since, to distinguish in Ireland between shadow and substance. And such comments may also help to explain why Desmond failed to cooperate effectively with them, in spite of agreeing to such clauses as the following:

As no small enormities occur by the continual recourse of idle men of lewd demeanor, called rhymers, bards, and dice players, called "carroghes," who, under pretense of their travail, bring privy intelligence between the malefactors inhabiting those shires to the great destruction of all true subjects, care should be taken that none of those sects, nor other evil persons, be suffered to travel within their rules; and that proclamation be made that whosoever should maintain such idle men within their territories should pay such fines as the President [of Munster] or Commissioners should think fit.

And as those rhymers by their ditties and rhymes, made for divers lords and gentlemen in Ireland, in commendation and high praise of extortion, rebellion, rape, rapine, and other injustice, encourage those lords rather to follow those vices than to abandon them, and for the making of such rhymes rewards are given by the gentlemen; for the abolition of so heinous an abuse, order should be taken with the said Earl, the lords and gentlemen, that henceforth they do not give any manner of reward for any such lewd rhymes, under pain of forfeiting double the sum they should so pay, and that the rhymers should be fined according to the discretion of the Commissioners.[80]

The only thing to be said for these terms is that they were easy ones compared with those which Spenser and Moryson, a generation later, proposed. The destructive element in Anglicization is perhaps best illustrated by such examples. Yet the need to transform Irish society is explicit in by far the larger number of surviving English commentaries.

Philip Sidney visited Ireland briefly in 1576, while his father was still Lord Deputy there, and from the wisdom of his twenty-two years prescribed for Ireland for the Queen's benefit. Answering the rhetorical question whether lenience or severity should be used in dealing with the Irish, he says, complacently and somewhat conventionally:

Truly, the general nature of all countries not fully conquered is against it. For until by time they find the sweetness of due subjection, it is impossible that any gentle means should put out the fresh remembrance of their lost liberty. And that the Irishman is that way as obstinate as any nation with whom no other passion can prevail but fear, besides their story, which plainly paint[s] it out, their manner of life, wherein they choose rather all filthiness than any law, and their own consciences, who best know their own natures, give sufficient proof of. For under the sun there is not a nation which live[s] more tyrannously than they do, one over the other.[81]

Richard Stanyhurst, taking a more sober view than, say, Philip Sidney, set out the minimum social objectives which an English conquest appeared to imply:

A conquest draweth, or at the leastwise ought to draw, to it three things, to wit law, apparel, and language. For where the country is subdued, there the inhabitants ought to be ruled by the same law that the conqueror is governed [by], to wear the same fashion of attire wherewith the victor is vested, and speak the same language that the vanquisher parleth. And if any of these three lack, doubtless the conquest limpeth.[82]

But this went well beyond what Irish lords and soldiers, and the learned classes associated with them, were willing, peacefully, to accept.

CHAPTER VI

Ireland as Arcadia

THE good qualities of the island, apart from its people, may be found magnified in many English writings. Thus Thomas Smith the younger writes of it (and more specifically of part of County Down) as

a land that floweth with milk and honey, a fertile soil truly if there be any in Europe, whether it be manured to corn or left to grass. There is timber, stone, plaster, and slate commodious for building everywhere abundant, a country full of springs, rivers, and lakes, both small and great, full of excellent fish and fowl.[1]

Robert Payne tells his readers that "it is not so hot in summer as England, neither is it so cold in winter." Parts of County Limerick he describes as "the gardens of the land for the variety and great plenty of all grain and fruits, and also there is more plenty of venison, fish, and fowl there than elsewhere in Ireland, although in every place there is great store."[2] In scores of other papers, mostly unpublished but circulated at the time, are similar comments on the fertility of Ireland, the fine quality of its timber, its rivers swarming with fish, its fields with game, its climate mild, its people (only) savage. But these eulogies are almost wholly to be found in propagandist tracts devoted to setting out the attractions of Ireland for English settlers. They are

58

perhaps at times sincere and objective, but they are all, true or false, inflated or factual, to be treated as sales talks for would-be settlers or investors in settlement. They do not, in themselves, throw much light on what Englishmen thought of Ireland, only what they wished their countrymen to think of it.

Yet there is another side to the favorable view of Ireland held by some Englishmen. The pastoral convention in Renaissance literature might be a literary device that was predominantly artificial, but it contained a small element that was authentically felt, a desire for, or at least a feeling for, primitive simplicity in human relations and in the setting of human life. And so Arcadia, like Utopia, could be Somewhere. It was possible for it to be, in a few men's minds and for a short time, Ireland. Ireland could be thought of as unspoiled by the complexity and sophistication of urban England; its landscape primitive, its people barbarous, perhaps, but simple in their ways of living, the whole removed from daily life and from the usual problems of existence.

We find this attitude illustrated lightly but firmly in Gervase Markham's "New Metamorphosis." When telling how Apollo, in the guise of a horse, had transported the goddess Calvina aerially to Ireland—on her way, incidentally, to establish the town of Galway—he has Apollo say:

> Together let us pass
> Into the bordering land of Bernia,
> There to the kingdom of Connaught,
> Which opposite doth lie, on th'other side
> The sea. No hissing serpent there doth bide,
> No toad, nor spider, adder, nor yet snake,
> No stinging venom'd thing may there partake
> The sweets and pleasures of that happy soil.
> There do they live without or tare or toil:
> They neither plant nor sow, nor till the ground,
> Nor with a hedge their own encompass round.

> All things are common; there they nothing want;
> They feel no penury or pinching scant.[3]

But Ireland could not, for Markham, who had campaigned there shortly before he wrote these verses, long sustain its role of never-never land.

The same sense of not quite real freedom to be experienced in Ireland is found here and there in Spenser, but with a background of feeling for the moods and rigors of the Irish landscape which goes much deeper than Markham, beyond the men, and the works of men, to be seen in it.[4]

Spenser showed Ireland as she was both before and after her fall from heavenly grace:

> Whilom when Ireland flourished in fame
>   Of wealths and goodness, far above the rest
>   Of all that bear the British Islands' name,
>   The Gods then us'd (for pleasure and for rest)
>   Oft to resort thereto, when seem'd them best:
>   But none of all therein more pleasure found,
>   Than Cynthia, that is sovereign Queen profest
>   Of woods and forest which therein abound,
> Sprinkled with wholesome waters, more than most on ground.

But Cynthia and Diana both turned against their playground island after Faunus had seen Diana bathing naked in the stream:

> Nathless Diana, full of indignation,
>   Thenceforth abandoned her delicious brook;
>   In whose sweet stream, before that bad occasion,
>   So much delight to bathe her limbs she took:
>   Ne only her, but also quite forsook
>   All those fair forests about Arlo hid,
>   And all that Mountain, which doth overlook
>   The richest champain that may else be rid,
> And the fair Shure, in which are thousand salmons bred.

Them all, and all that she so dear did weigh,
  Thenceforth she left; and parting from the place,
  Thereon an heavy hapless curse did lay,
  To weet, that wolves, where she was wont to space,
  Should harbor'd be and all those woods deface,
  And thieves should rob and spoil that coast around:
  Since which those woods, and all that goodly chase
  Doth to this day with woods and thieves abound:
Which too-too true that land's indwellers since have found.[5]

Yet Spenser did not go on to make the point that Munster had had to be ruined and devastated before it could be seized for English settlers ("indwellers") to occupy, or indeed that the thieves, or many of them, were a product of English conquest.

These indications are slight, but they help to make the point that however much Englishmen might find Irish life incomprehensible to them and so in need of improvement, and Irishmen tiresome if not more positively objectionable, there was at the same time something about Ireland and the Irish which they found attractive. Perhaps it was merely that both country and people were so different from England: they formed a mirror in which something strange could be seen. The love-hate relationship, which so much of the English commentary reveals, can perhaps provide matter for the sociologist to probe. The casual observer can scarcely take it further.

CHAPTER VII

A Way of Life Anatomized

THE English observer not only concerned himself with institutions but with people: he found the habits of the Irish even more worthy of description than their political and social relationships. There is in the accounts of how people lived and ate and diverted themselves the same combination of straight description, qualified by misunderstandings from time to time, and hostile bias, which is more pronounced on the personal than on the institutional plane. As John Derricke put it, neatly for him, "My soul doth detest their wild shamrock manners." [1] The same urge to characterize and reform (or control) which we have noticed already was there, as we see from Captain Henry Ackworth's letter to Lord Burghley in 1574. He spoke of the Irish as "this simple subtle people," before going on to advocate that the Queen should "bridle these unruly Irish colts with a sharp English bit." [2] Much of what is said is of great interest to students of folklore and of social anthropology. Only a little of this commentary has been evaluated by serious students. Far too much has survived for more than a small selection of topics to be illustrated in a cursory treatment, but, slight as they are, they carry the Irishman forward on English words from birth to death.

The more truly pastoral parts of the country, in the North and West, were so bound up with the life of the animals the people tended that their primary foods were flesh and animal products. Barnaby Rich despised the Irish country people because they did not eat bread made from wheat or rye but contented themselves with oatcakes, which he found unattractive to see and to eat, being flat and hard. He complained too that they were cindery because of the way in which the grain had been cleaned.[3] Moryson tells us that "the foresaid wild Irish do not thresh their oats but burn them from the straw." [4] He, like Rich, regarded this custom as dirty and a sign of Irish ineffectiveness. It was, no doubt, an ancient custom, but it is likely to have been found throughout the Atlantic fringe of Europe, where oats provided the primary cereal. Moreover, in Ireland the technique of tapping out the grain at the precise moment when it would fall from the burning hull was a highly skilled one. The object was to provide the freshest possible grain for baking, since by its use the oats could rapidly appear at table after baking in the form of "quickbread," which was regarded as having the best flavor.[5] Rich and Moryson, indeed, though they were right in regarding this as a primitive custom, were quite wrong in thinking that it did not have its own kind of sophistication.

Moryson also found Irish practices in grinding corn in the ancient querns strange—and unpleasant also, though he is involved here in the lesser reticences of a pastoral-based society. He says, "At Cork I have seen with these eyes young maids, stark naked, grinding of corn with certain stones to make cakes thereof." [6] This was probably a very sensible practice for people accustomed to wearing heavy woolen garments, which otherwise would be covered with and damaged by the meal. But Moryson found the practice of these girls, "striking off into the tub of meal such reliques thereof as stuck on their belly, thighs, and more unseemly parts," [7] repugnant, though he would probably not have turned a hair had an English miller flicked flour from his jerkin or apron into the sack. The fact that grain was eaten so little in the oat-growing areas surprised him too, though this is not strange. Oats, and barley also, were, as he admits, required basically as horse fodder, then (in the case of barley) for making whiskey, and only residually for human consumption. Moryson says of the oatcakes: "They seldom eat this bread, much less any better kind." [8] The Bohemian baron, whom he quotes several times, "first landed among them in the furthest north [in O Cahan's country, as we shall see], where for eight days' space he had found no bread, not so much as a cake of oats, till he came to eat with the Earl of Tyrone [at Dungannon?] and . . . related this their want of bread to us for a miracle." Indeed, Moryson went on to state that even in peacetime the Irish "impute covetousness and base birth to him that hath any corn after Christmas." [9] It is most unlikely that this extreme attitude would be found in the south or central parts of Ireland except in time of war when grain crops would be hard to harvest, but nothing he records so sharply illustrates the pastoral emphasis of the old Gaelic order. Francisco Cuellar, shipwrecked in County Sligo from the Spanish Armada, was, in extremity, sent a meal by an Irish girl of "butter and milk and a small piece of oaten bread to eat." [10] The order in which these commodities are mentioned indicates their respective quantities.

If we continue to remember that the diet of the Irish sprang largely from their pastoral heritage, much of what Fynes Moryson says about their other food products makes sense. After pointing out that bread was seldom eaten, he goes on to say that the Irish "drink milk like nectar, warmed with a stone first cast into the fire, or else beef-broth mingled with milk." They take the calves away from the cows "that themselves may have more abundance of milk," while "they love no meat more than sour milk curdled," and "esteem for a great dainty sour curds, vulgarly called by them Bonaclabbe[r] [*bainne clabair*]." [11] Perhaps this was why Rich found that it was thought unlucky and "a presagement of some misfortune to keep their milking vessels cleanly," [12] since otherwise the milk would not sour so quickly.

They also made much butter (they kept it in wooden vessels buried in the bog against a time of shortage), and, says Moryson, "they swallow lumps of butter mixed with oatmeal, and often let their cows' blood, eating the congealed blood with butter," [13] which both Stanyhurst and Good [14] tell us made a jelly-like food.

The Irish were flesh eaters. Moryson says they "most commonly eat flesh, many times raw; and if it be roasted or sodd [boiled], they seldom eat bread with it" [15] (as he has said before), yet, paradoxically, he says too, "they will not kill a cow, except it be old and yield no milk," [16] a typical pastoralist reaction, especially in the spring and summer. Also, "they seldom eat wildfowl or fish, though they have great plenty of both," adding that this was due to Irish laziness—"the fishermen must be beaten out before they will go to their boats," [17] though he cites Irish hunting practices which do not quite agree with his previous conclusions.[18] He insists that many of the Irish "eat no flesh, but that which dies of disease or otherwise of itself, neither can it escape them for stinking. . . . Yea, . . . they will feed on horses dying of themselves, not only upon small want of flesh, but even for pleasure." Lord Mountjoy is even said to have found that a soldier who cut off the rumps of dead horses was one of the "English-Irish," not even "mere Irish." He boldly told the Lord Deputy, "Your Lordship may please to eat pheasant and partridge, and much good do it you, that best likes your taste; and I hope it is lawful for me without offense to eat this flesh that likes me better than beef." [19] Though dangerously decayed carrion may have been eaten in time of starvation, the countryman knew enough about flesh not to eat dangerous meat under normal conditions. "They devour great morsels of beef unsalted, and they eat commonly swine's flesh, seldom mutton," while many calves were killed and stewed, "being nothing but froth," says Moryson,[20] making veal-eating appear distasteful. Stanyhurst admitted that "flesh they devour without bread and that half raw." [21] He adds that "no meat they fancy so much as pork, and the fatter the better. One of John [Shane] O Neill's household demanded of his fellow whether beef were better than pork? 'That,' quoth the other, 'is as intricate a question as to ask whether thou art better than O Neill.'"

Moryson had great contempt for Irish kitchen practices: "They scum the seething pot with an handful of straw, and strain their milk taken from the cow through a like handful of straw, none of the cleanest, and so cleanse, or rather more defile, the pot and milk." [22] Much of the cooking was done by stewing meat in the beast's skin strung from a rough framework over a slow fire, illustrated—as we shall see—by John Derricke. Moryson spoke of the "filthy poke" in which veal was boiled, and of "the hollow tree, lapped in a raw cow's hide," in which were put "pieces of flesh, as also the entrails of beasts unwashed," and which was "set over the fire" to "seethe." [23] "They desire no broth," he says (though we have seen him talk of a beef broth with milk), "nor have any use of a spoon." They did not, it seems, care to cook vegetables, if what he says is correct, that "they can neither seethe artichokes nor eat them when they are sodden." [24] At the same time, "They gladly eat raw herbs, as watercresses and shamrocks," [25] the latter being almost certainly wood sorrel, not the clovers known later as shamrock, as his other rather ludicrous picture shows: "They willingly eat the herb shamrock, being of a sharp taste, which, as they run and are chased to and fro, they snatch like beasts out of the ditches." [26] Father Good noted, more dispassionately, "They feed willingly upon herbs and watercresses, especially upon mushrooms, shamroots [as he writes it] and roots." [27] Stanyhurst equated "shamrocks" with watercress but said they also ate other herbs and roots.[28]

Dietetically, the Irish food was well balanced, and the combination of salad greens with high protein foods seems more than adequate by modern standards, much better than foods enjoyed by bread-eating peasants, many of whom got little in the way of meat products over a good part of the year. Indeed this may be demonstrated by repeated English emphasis on Irish physique. Some of Moryson's strictures against Irish kitchen practices may have been the result of his assuming a high standard of behavior to impress his readers, others, the result of ignorance: he evidently did not realize that the countryman with, for example, a wisp of firm oat or rye straw, could use it as a clean and satisfactory strainer. Cooking in the hide, a very ancient survival no doubt, was not unhygienic and was convenient when the Irish were moving about or were in their summer pastures, where they would not need to be bothered with metal vessels, which they had had, of course, since the Bronze Age. It is likely that some Irish cooking and eating practices were also dirty and inelegant, but so were those, no doubt, of other countrymen: the townsman alone had the time and circumstances to refine household practice and abundant utensils and servants to assist him, even though a town kitchen in Elizabethan England was probably also in many cases a noisome place.

One Irish product for which Englishmen had little but praise was usquebaugh (*uisce beathadh,* aqua vitae). Irish whiskey, though it was said by Luke Gernon to owe something of its quality to added licorice,[29] and by Moryson to "raisins, fennelseed, and other things," [30] was regarded by Gernon as "a very wholesome drink and natural to digest the crudities of Irish feeding. You may drink a naggin without offense, which is the fourth part of a pint." Sir Josias Bodley, when he was in Lecale in 1603, also convinced himself that whiskey was "pre-eminently wholesome in these regions, where the priests themselves . . . pour usquebaugh down their throats by day and by night." [31] Moryson, censorious of so much in Ireland, gives it almost unqualified praise as "the best in the world in that kind," [32] but the Irish and Old English alike, he thought, both men and women (the latter he professed to find rather shocking), drank whiskey in too great quantities. Good says they "pour down the throat . . . draft after draft." [33] Indeed, Stanyhurst admitted as much, saying that in the Irish parts of the island it was swilled down after one of their heavy meals "by quarts and pottles." [34] Stanyhurst was most partial of all to it: "it is a sovereign liquor if it be orderly taken," but then he had been brought up in Dublin, where, indeed, his remarks on whiskey were reprinted in 1961.[35] To English soldiers, Irish whiskey, therefore, provided some consolation during their uncomfortable conquering campaigns.

The most sensitive area of Irish life touched by the English commentators was that of personal habits and hygiene. Dirt, lice, fleas, and smells were characteristic of much European town and country life in the sixteenth century. On the other hand, the upper classes set some store on personal hygiene as part of the code of good-mannerly relations laid down in the courtesy books which had such a prominent place in the educational literature of the Renaissance. Where, therefore, Barnaby Rich calls attention to "the sluttish and uncleanly observations of the Irish," [36] and Fynes Moryson says, "the wild Irish . . . are barbarous and most filthy in their diet," [37] it is hard to say precisely how objective they were attempting to be. Both Rich and Moryson show themselves to be strongly prejudiced against Irish ways of living, though this does not, especially in the case of Moryson, curb their curiosity. Moryson, too, is desirous of being thought the gentleman and had the background of his European travels to instruct him: it is probable that at times at least he is engaged in exaggerating his own gentility at the expense of the people he observed. It can also be shown that both observers recorded more accurately than they assessed and understood certain Irish practices which arose out of the pastoral heritage and the tenacious adhesion to custom. Rich is quite correct in stressing the latter feature: "Custom is a metal amongst them that standeth which way soever it be bent. Check them for their uncleanliness and they plead custom." He went on, characteristically, to complain that "they are deaf to all good counsels," [38] that is, to the acceptance of English habits instead of their own.

Ireland had, indeed, especially with physicians, a bad reputation for the infestation of its people with lice. Andrew Boorde, doctor and cleric, illustrated the Irish by a woodcut (Plate 9) showing an Irishwoman amiably delousing the head of a kern or horseboy, who is identified by his characteristic dart and by the verse:

> Pediculus [the louse] otherwhile do bite me by the back,
> Wherefore divers times I make their bones crack.[39]

Again, writing about 1590, Dr. Thomas Moffet says, "all Ireland is noted for this, that it swarms almost with lice," and attributes this to "the beastliness of the people and want of cleanly women to wash them," considering that "the English [he seems to mean the Old English], that are more careful to dress themselves, changing and washing their shirts often, having inhabited so long in Ireland, have escaped that plague." [40] The Irish louse, indeed, becomes an English figure of fun. Joseph Hall, in *The Discovery of a New World* (1609), written around the turn of the reigns, says of a series of insignificant distances, "They all make but a day's journey for an Irish louse, be she never so speedy." [41] Moryson is at his most censorious when speaking on this subject:

And let no man wonder that they are lousy, for never any barbarous people were found in all kinds more slovenly than they are. And nothing is more common among them than for the men to lie upon the women's laps on green hills till they kill their lice, with a strange nimbleness proper to that nation.[42]

Spenser spoke especially of the "going women":

And as for all other good women which love to do but little work, how handsome it is to lie in [their mantles] and sleep or to louse themselves in the sunshine they that have been but a while in Ireland can well witness.[43]

How far the Irish men and women who wandered the roads can have been at all typical of the rest it is hard to say; nor do we know how far lice were confused with sheep ticks and animal fleas which many Irish people could scarcely avoid.

It is, indeed, very likely—though here one can only guess to what degree—that many of the Irish, in the outlying parts of the country at least, were not at all cleanly in their personal habits. The Irishman lived close to his animals. When they needed it, they found shelter beside him, either in his winter or his summer dwelling. The Irish "lodge in the same house, if it may be called a house, with their beasts," as Moryson has it.[44] Through the summer booleys, built of sods of turf or wickerwork faced with sods and roofed with branches and heather—as Professor Estyn Evans describes them [45]—the cows passed in turn from front door to back while they were being milked. In the normal countryman's winter house, whether it was rectangular or circular in layout—it varied in different parts of the country—the livestock crowded in with the family, as in so many other peasant communities in northern and western Europe. The lighting in the Irish house was poor: "They . . . place," says Moryson, "a great candle made of reeds and butter upon the floor in the midst of a great room," while "the chief men in their houses make fires in the midst of the room, the smoke whereof goeth out at a hole in the top thereof"—or largely failed, as others said, to go out. He adds sarcastically, "I trust no man expects among these gallants any beds, much less feather beds and sheets." Their sleeping customs appear strange to his eyes:

They make a fire in the midst of the room, and round about it they sleep upon the ground, without straw or other thing under them, lying all in a circle about the fire with their feet toward it. And their bodies being naked, they cover their heads and upper parts with their mantles, which they first make very wet, steeping them in water of purpose, for they find that when their bodies have once warmed the wet mantles the smoke of them keeps their bodies in temperate heat all the night following.[46]

Modern commentators have found confirmation for these descriptions,[47] except for the damp mantles, but even this sounds like the fruit of observation.

Moryson records that the Irish, when moving to their summer pastures, "sleep under the canopy of heaven." He characterizes their winter and summer homes respectively as "a poor cabin made of clay" and "a cabin made of the boughs of trees and covered with turf," concluding, "Such are the dwellings of the very lords among them." [48] But while there is nothing necessarily untrue about this, it is clearly not a generalization applicable to anything like the whole of Gaelic Ireland, in many parts of which stone houses were built both for winter and summer use. It seems, as does so much of the English commentary which stresses the extreme primitiveness of Irish life, to rely largely on descriptions of the territories of the O Neills and their dependents in Ulster. At the same time, it is a recurrent complaint that the Irish "live brutishly all in a cott, or rather a sty, more like beasts than men." [49]

For his part, the Irish lord kept open house, as may be seen from the experience in 1601 of a Bohemian nobleman, Jaroslav z Donína, Baron of Dohna,[50] who traveled through Scotland to the North of Ireland, visiting Hugh O Neill, Earl of Tyrone, then at war against the English, before returning to London to report his experiences to Sir Robert Cecil and Queen Elizabeth. Fynes Moryson tells graphically how:

He coming to the house of Ocane [Donnell O Cahan, Irish lord of part of modern County Londonderry], a great lord among them, was met at the door with sixteen women, all naked, excepting their loose mantles; whereof eight or ten were very fair and two seemed very

Nymphs. With which strange sight his eyes being dazzled, they led him into the house, and there sitting down by the fire, with crossed legs like tailors, and so low as could not but offend chaste eyes, desired him to sit down with them. Soon after, Ocane, the Lord of the Country, came in all naked except a loose mantle and shoes, which he put off as soon as he came in, and, entertaining the Baron after his best manner in the Latin tongue, desired him to put off his apparel, which he thought to be a burden to him, and to sit naked by the fire with this naked company. But the Baron, when he came to himself after some astonishment at this strange sight, professed that he was so inflamed therewith as for shame he durst not put off his apparel.

How far the old types of earthen enclosure (*ráth, lios, dún*), of which so many examples survive in Ireland, continued in the sixteenth century to be employed either for habitation or for the safeguarding of cattle will not be known until more excavation has been done.[51] The Ulstermen still used the lake dwelling on an artificial island (*crannóg*) as a place of refuge. It is clear that in the West the defensive, circular, stone-walled enclosure (*caiseal, cathair*) continued in use. In County Clare it might, indeed, be equipped with a new fortified gatehouse. In Ulster, much of the building, defensive or domestic, was in timber. But the most prominent stone building of the greater part of Gaelic Ireland by the sixteenth century was the tower house.[52] Copied in the Irish areas from the towers developed by the Old English, these were built in great numbers from the middle of the fifteenth to the end of the sixteenth century. Over one thousand castles have been enumerated in the western coastal counties from Cork to Donegal:[53] possibly five hundred of these were Irish tower houses, perhaps more. These fortified residences were strong enough to resist attack, yet they could normally be used as living rather than garrison accommodation. Over a cellar and a first (ground) floor containing domestic offices, they comprised a large hall on the second floor and sleeping chambers above on one or two further floors, with perhaps accommodation above these again for sentinels and servants in the attics contained within the parapets. Rather dark, as they could have few windows, and served only by a steep stone stair, they nevertheless combined security with some degree of civilized comfort. It is significant that in plan and in detail they differ little between the Old English areas of, say, Kilkenny and Wexford, and the Irish areas of West Cork, Kerry, and Clare, though the former are on the average, perhaps, larger and more complex in plan. Yet Irish lords like the O Briens were also building larger and more complex castles, like Bunratty, County Clare, in the fifteenth century. To them were also joined large wooden or clay-walled halls, annexes for the large lordly households.

We have two word pictures which give us some conception of how the tower houses and their appended buildings appeared to contemporaries, the first from Stanyhurst, the second from Moryson.

Thus these lords (always I except O Neill, who rules in Ulster, for he is a strong adversary of British rule and keeps his courts in fields of herbage) have castles well fortified and strongly built of stone. To them are joined halls, spacious and large enough, built of a mixture of clay and mud. They are not firmly roofed with slate or rough-hewn stone or tile but are usually thatched with straw from the fields. In these halls they usually dine, yet they rarely sleep in them, because their enemies may easily apply fiery torches to the halls, the material of which, inflamed by the wind, takes fire rapidly.[54]

Many gentlemen have castles built of freestone unpolished and of flints or little stones, and they are built strong for defense in times of rebellion, for which cause they have narrow stairs and little windows, and commonly they have a spacious hall joining to the castle and built of timber and clay, wherein they eat with their family. Neither are many of these gentlemen's houses void of filth and slovenliness.[55]

73

The same two writers stress—and it is likely that Moryson in both cases used Stanyhurst as a model for his description—the large enclosure which marked the older type of stone fort, Stanyhurst stressing the size of the area it enclosed,[56] Moryson emphasizing its primitiveness: "For other Irish dwellings, it may be said of them as Caesar said of the old Britons' houses. They call it a town when they have compassed a skirt of wood with trees cut down, whither they may retire themselves and their cattle." [57]

What neither brings out clearly is that the tower houses were themselves usually surrounded by a walled enclosure, the bawn. This is mentioned only incidentally by Fynes Moryson where he says, "The cattle . . . are brought at evening within the bawns of castles where they stand or lie all night in a dirty yard." [58] The Irish *cathair* might itself hold the cattle, or they might be dispersed in an outer enclosure around it. The hill forts were usually summer or emergency enclosures only, perhaps guarded by men who did not live inside the enclosed area but merely looked after it from without. They might have within them the lightly built shelters characteristic of the period of transhumance.

There is apparently no detailed English description of life in an Irish tower house for the Elizabethan period, but Tadhg Dall Ó Huiginn (1550–1591) gives an attractive picture of Lifford Castle, County Donegal, built by Manus O Donnell in 1527:

A beloved dwelling is the castle of Lifford, homestead of a wealth-abounding encampment; forge of hospitality for the men of Ulster, a dwelling it is hard to leave. . . .

Beloved the delightful, lofty building, its tables, its coverlets, its cupboards; its wondrous, handsome, firm walls, its smooth marble arches.

Beloved is the castle in which we used to spend a while at chess-playing, a while with the daughters of the men of Bregia, a while with the fair books of the poets.

A Way of Life Anatomized

The fortress of smooth-lawned Lifford—no one in the world can leave it once it is found.[59]

The castle built by the traveled Manus O Donnell was probably more elaborate than most of those built by the northern lords, and perhaps, too, poetic license has glorified it unduly, but the poem provides a background for the Jacobean description by Luke Gernon of a castle he had been to in the Southwest about 1620, which is probably referable, without too much alteration, to Elizabethan times:

We are come to the castle already. The castles are built very strong, and with narrow stairs for security. The hall is the uppermost room. Let us go up; you shall not come down again till tomorrow. . . . The lady of the house meets you with her train. . . . Salutations past, you shall be presented with all the drinks in the house, first the ordinary beer, then aqua vitae, then sack, then old ale: the lady tastes it, you must not refuse it. The fire is prepared in the middle of the hall, where you may solace yourself till suppertime. . . . By this time the table is spread and plentifully furnished with variety of meats, but ill cooked and without sauce. Neither shall there be wanting a pasty or two of red deer. . . . The dish which I make choice of is the swelled mutton. . . . I make choice of it to avoid uncleanly dressing. They feast together with great jollity and healths around. Toward the middle of supper the harper begins to tune and singeth Irish rhymes of ancient making. If he be a good rhymer he will make one song to the present occasion. Supper being ended, it is your liberty to sit up or to depart to your lodging: you shall have company in both kind. When you come to your chamber, do not expect canopy and curtains. It is very well if your bed content you, and, if the company be great, you may happen to be bodkin in the middle. In the morning there will be brought unto you a cup of aqua vitae. . . . Breakfast is but the repetition of supper. When you are disposing of yourself to depart, they call for a Dogh a dores [deoch an dorais, a stirrup-cup]. . . . There you are presented again with all the drinks in the house, as at your first entrance. Smack them over and let us depart.[60]

In this sprightly account, the horrors of Irish hospitality are considerably mitigated from the Elizabethan depths as Moryson described them; perhaps this was not due so much to change in Irish ways as to an alteration in tone on the part of the English visitor.

In English opinion, a basic defect of Irish agrarian life was that it conduced to laziness and, indeed, to dissipation. Tending cows and horses seemed to Fynes Moryson an easy excuse for not doing harder labor in the fields. This easygoing habit of life, he considered, had even infected the Old English who came into contact with it. He says:

The Irish thus given to idleness, naturally abhor from manual arts and civil trades to gain their own bread. . . . For whereas all, yea the most strong and able bodies, and men given to spoils and robberies in all times, gladly employed themselves in feeding of cows, that course of life was embraced by them as suitable to their innate sloth and as most fit to elude or protract all execution of justice against them, while they commonly lived in thick woods abounding with grass.[61]

Spenser was equally forthright: "This keeping of cows is of itself a very idle life and a fit nursery for a thief." He would "not mean to allow any of these able bodies, which are able to use bodily labor, to follow a few cows grazing, but such impotent persons, as, being unable for strong travail, are yet able to drive cattle to and fro the pasture." [62] This and similar comments by others are characteristic reactions of men brought up in a corn-growing rural economy. Tillage and the horticulture which supplemented it made up a full-time occupation. Pastoralism imposed heavy tasks at some seasons and bound men to the natural rhythms of their own animals (milking times, for example), but it was not in many parts of Ireland, even though it was supplemented by a greater or lesser amount of cultivation, a full-time occupation all the year round. Nor is it surprising that

Moryson thought "less grazing and more tillage" [63] was the cure for Irish restlessness, together with the creation of tenancies on the English model, with English landlords to supervise them, the main social benefit to be expected from colonization.

At the same time, an aristocratic society did indeed tend to make some of its members lazy. The soldiery easily turned into "idlemen" when there was no fighting to be done. Men and women with any claim to aristocratic descent—very many in Ireland—flaunted it by insisting on doing as little as possible. Father Good was another who saw idleness as a general characteristic: "Given they are to idleness above all things; they reckon it the greatest riches to take no pain and count it the most pleasure to enjoy liberty." [64] Rich singles out the women: "To speak truth of our gentlewomen of Ireland that be of Irish birth, they have little practice either in pride or in good huswifery, for they are for the most part always busied in taking their ease, and it is holden for a servile kind of baseness amongst the Irish for a gentleman or a gentlewoman to be seen in any manner of faculty, idleness only excepted." [65] It is not easy to reconcile this statement with Spenser's: "The Irishwomen [have] the trust and care of all things, both at home and in the fields," [66] though perhaps this was only in plebeian households. Spenser, indeed, had seen more of the Irish of the settled areas of the East and South than a good many other observers, and he paid tribute to the peasantry as hard-working plowmen: "The country people themselves are great plowers and small spenders." [67] His aim was to turn the "idlemen" into as useful members of society as the peasants. It would seem to follow from this that Moryson's lazy cow-minder was not typical of the Irish peasantry as a whole.

Like many peasantries, the Irish would work long and hard for part of the year but relax wholly at other times. One such occasion occurred when they left their oatfields and meadows and pastures for the towns of the Old English coast lands. Fynes

Moryson points the contrast in their behavior when they came with wealth in the shape of cattle to the towns:

For howsoever while they live in woods and in cabins with their cattle they could be content with water and milk, yet when they came to towns nothing was more frequent than to tie their cows at the doors, and never part from the taverns till they had drunk them out in sack and strong water, which they call usquebaugh; and this did not only the lords, but the common people, though half naked for want of clothes to cover them.[68]

"Plowing by the tail" [69] was another Irish custom which Rich and Moryson disapprovingly recorded. The former says:

In the plowing of their land . . . they used the labor of five several persons to every plow, and their team of cattle, which commonly consisted of five or six horses, were placed all in front, having neither cords, chains, nor lines whereby to draw, but every horse by his own tail. And this was the manner of plowing when I knew Ireland first [nearly forty years before 1610, when he was writing] and is used still at this day in many places of the country.[70]

Moryson writes:

The Irish used no harness or traces for horses drawing in the plough or drawing sledges with carriage, but only fastened the plough and the carriage by withes to the tails of the horses (or garrans [*gearráin*, nags] for so they call them), whereby the tails of them are commonly pulled off, and the very rumps bared.[71]

Both these descriptions are valuable for detail—the heavy labor force involved, the tying of the tails by willow twigs to the plow, the use of this method of traction as well for the slide cars which the Irish employed. What neither observer is correct in doing is implying that the Irish did not have, as well, a heavy plow pulled by harnessed horse- or ox-teams. The light, wooden tail plow was used only for replowed land and in thin soil was valuable in that the horses would stop when one of the frequent stones was met, and so the plowshare was saved and the plowman avoided injury. It seems that this method was also suitable for some of the steeper slopes on which land was cultivated or across which turf (for burning) was brought by car. It was a custom which lasted in the west of Ireland until the nineteenth century, but by that time rather from its antiquity as a cultural heritage than from its special utility.

Moryson realized that many Irish customs were very ancient and could be related to descriptions of pastoral societies in eastern Europe dating back to Roman times. Thus he says: "Yet will they upon hunger in time of war open a vein of the cow and drink the blood, but in no case kill or much weaken it. A man would think these men to be Scythians, who let their horses' blood under the ears, and for nourishment drink their blood." [72]

The emphasis by some writers on the insanitary habits of the Irish, the wild expression given to the men by their "glibs," and the general air of savagery which surrounded them, makes it, perhaps, surprising that the surviving illustrations are favorable evidence of their appearance, as we shall see, while there is also verbal evidence of the attractive looks of many of them and often complimentary comments on certain of their hygienic practices and on their manual dexterity. These are all remarked by Good when he is trying to place the Irish in their categories in the physiological framework of "humors":

That these Irish people are both of an hotter and moister nature than other nations we may well conjecture [the Irish were therefore "sanguine" in temperament]. And this we gather by their wonderful soft skin, which doubtless cometh as well by the nature of the soil as by certain artificial bathings and exercise that they use [bathing in stone troughs warmed by hot stones]. By reason also of the same tenderness of their muscles, they so excel in nimbleness and flexibility of all parts of the body as it is incredible.[73]

The English priest is echoed by Stanyhurst: "The men are clean of skin and hue, of stature tall. The women are well favored, clean-colored, fair-handed, big and large; suffered from their infancy to grow at will [that is, are uncorseted in youth]; nothing curious of their feature and proportion of body." [74] The Irish then emerge as less wholly unfavored in their persons than might, from some of the earlier passages cited, have been supposed.

Just as Irish rules of descent baffled and annoyed some Englishmen, so too did Irish matrimonial practices. Irish lords appear to have cohabited freely with women other than their wives, did little or nothing to discriminate against their illegitimate children, and even accepted on their death beds, we are told, the illegitimate children fathered on them not only by the promiscuous "going women" but by the wives of other men.[75] Nor was it always clear who at any one time was the lawful wedded wife of an Irish notability, or how long she would remain so. There are a number of comments,[76] mostly uncomplimentary ones, by English observers on the freedom with which marriages could be dissolved. The priests are represented as carrying on a steady, but not by any means wholly successful, campaign for lifelong monogamy. At the same time, candidates for Irish episcopal sees at Rome usually described themselves, according to Pope Gregory XIII, as "nobles and bastards." [77]

Father Good, writing as a priest, is probably a fairly reliable witness to the true state of affairs when he says:

Town dwellers seldom make any contract of marriage with them of the country, and these pass their promise not for [the] present but for the future time, or else give assent without deliberation. Whence it is that for every light falling out they part asunder, the husband to another woman, the wife to another husband. Neither is it ever known for certainty whether their contracts have been true or false before they give up their last gasp. Hence rise contentions about the possession of lands; hence grow robberies, depredations, manslaughters and deadly hatred. . . . For all of them are marvelously prone to incest [that is, cohabitation inside the prohibited degrees of the church], and nothing is there so common as divorces under pretense of conscience.[78]

Stanyhurst, however, indicates there had been some improvement, from the monogamist standpoint, owing to the priests, saying:

In old time they much abused the honorable state of marriage, either in contracts unlawful, meeting the degrees of prohibition, or in divorcements at pleasure, or in retaining concubines or harlots for wives. Yea, even at this day, where the clergy is faint, they can be content to marry for a year and a day of probation, and at the year's end or any time after to return her home with her marriage goods or as much in value, upon light quarrels, if the gentlewoman's friends be unable to revenge the injury. In like manner may she forsake her husband.[79]

It would seem that incompleted or contingent contracts of marriage, which included a form of trial marriage, together with allegations of consanguinity, were the usual causes for the dissolution of a marriage. Divorce, or annulment, was normally carried out by proceedings before the brehons, who investigated the character of the contract and the distribution of the damages to be paid by the injured party. Sir William Pelham hoped in 1580 in Munster "to shake off their most damnable custom of taking and repudiating their wives." [80] Divorce was not, however, quite as easy (except perhaps for someone as powerful as O Neill) as Moryson would indicate: "The mere Irish divorced wives, and with their consent took them again frequently, and for small, yea ridiculous, causes, always paying a bribe of cows [correctly, a fee] to the Brehon judges and sending the wife away with some few cows more than she brought." [81] He adds a number of tales, one of which will indicate his attitude:

I could name a great lord among them, who was credibly reported to have put away his wife of a good family and beautiful, only for a fault as light as wind (which the Irish in general abhor [there are many references to the Irish objection to farting]), but I dare not name it, lest I offend the perfumed senses of some whose censure I have incurred in that kind.[82]

The wandering women were remarked on by Smyth as "a sort of woman that be called the going women: they be great blasphemers of God, and they run from country to country, sowing sedition amongst the people. They are common to all men." [83] Spenser, in the course of his great diatribe on the Irish mantle, says that for

these wandering women, called by them "Monashut [*mná siubhail*]," it is half a wardrobe. For in summer ye shall find her arrayed commonly but in her smock and mantle to be more ready for her light services. In winter and in her travel it is her cloak and safeguard, and also a coverlet for her lewd exercise. And when she hath filled her vessel, under it she can hide both her burden and her blame. Yea, and when her bastard is born, it serves instead of all her swaddling clouts, her mantles [being] her cradles, with which others are vainly cumbered.[84]

The Irishman, we understand from English observers, was born easily and lay on his deathbed listening to the jokes and laughter of his friends. His death was marked by loud outcries which accompanied the mourning ceremonies until his burial. Thus Moryson tells us that:

Touching child-bearing, women within two hours after they are delivered, many times leave their beds to go sop and drink with women coming to visit them. . . . Some say that commonly the women have little or no pain in child-bearing. . . . No doubt they have such easy deliverance, and commonly such strange ability of body presently after it, as I never heard any woman in the world to have the like. . . . Midwives and neighbours come to help women to be delivered commonly more for fashion than any great need of them.[85]

Of the other end of life, Moryson remarked that on their deathbeds there was no talk of wills (as all was settled by law and custom) or of repentance (as considered bad for the patient), "but all their speeches tend to mirth and hope of recovery; and the sick person hath about him many lights and great show of company, as if thereby they could keep him from death." But when a man asks for the sacrament they take it "for a desperate sign of death." At this point "the near friends and all the company call and cry out to him, . . . reproaching him with unkindness in forsaking them, and asking whither and to whom he will go to be in better case than he is with them." Finally, "when the sick person is dead they make a monstrous cry, with shrieking, howling, and clamping of hands; and in like sort they follow the dead body at the burial, in which outcries the nurse, the daughters and the concubines are most vehement." [86] Father Good also remarked the Irish keen (*caoine*) at their mourning ceremonies,[87] while Spenser regarded "their lamentations at their burials, with despairful outcries and immoderate wailings" as "altogether heathenish" and exhibiting their affinities with the ancient Scythians.[88] Stanyhurst thought these "howling and barbarous outcries" were the origin of the proverbial phrase "to weep Irish," [89] though Rich considered that "to weep Irish is to weep at pleasure." [90]

Throughout, one can find examples where English writers at the same time record somewhat scornfully Irish traditionalism and express their admiration for Irish fortitude in face of death. Examples were often taken from Irishmen who were undergoing torture or were being executed for opposing the Queen. Thus Bacon, in his essay "Of Custom and Education," says, "I remember, in the beginning of Queen Elizabeth's time of England, an Irish rebel condemned, put up a petition to the Deputy that he be hanged in a with [a willow twig] and not in an halter; because it had been so used with former rebels." [91] Joseph Hall took his example of proud Irish fortitude from a similar occasion: "I have heard of an Irish traitor that when he lay pining upon the wheel with his bones broke, asked his friend if he changed his countenance at all, caring less for the pain than the show of fear." [92]

If the Irishman's ties were to his own "name" and to the lord of his *tuath*, whether or not he bore his name, almost all English observers remarked the strength of the artificial ties of fosterage. Again, Moryson is our clearest source:

They seldom nurse their own children, especially the wives of lords and gentlemen. . . . For women of good wealth seek with great ambition to nurse them, not for any profit, rather spending much upon them while they live, and giving them when they die sometimes more than to their own children. But they do it only to have the protection and love of the parents whose children they nurse.

And old custom is so turned into a second nature with them as they esteem the children they nurse more than their own, holding it a reproach to nurse their own children. Yea, men will forbear their wives' bed for the good of the children they nurse or foster, but not nursing their own. Yea, the foster brothers . . . love one another better than natural brothers. . . . The worst is that these nurses with their extreme indulgence corrupt the children they foster, nourishing and heartening the boys in all villainy, and the girls in obscenity.[93]

Campion said that Turloch Luineach O Neill was more attached to his foster brothers than to his own.[94] But the worst danger of fosterage, Spenser [95] and others were sure, was its Hibernicizing effects on the Old English who practiced it in association with their Irish neighbors.

It is amusing to discover that, even after conquest and the arrival of many New English colonists, fosterage was taken over by them and was soon condemned by reformers as a dangerous means of enticing children away from good English to bad Irish ways of life, one of them saying:

The fostering of children with Irish nurses is a main inconvenience both in respect of religion, manners, and language, for thereby they grow wholly up into their customs, study how to cozen the new-come English, build their houses without chimneys, come stooping out of their doors, which they build low to keep out the trooper's horse, denies himself when he is within and what not. And this Englishman's son, begotten or fostered among the Irish, will first grow a stranger to his own father and brothers in comparison of the affection he beareth to his fosterers, and in short time will grow adverse in affection to the government of the state, and come there peace, come there war, he will be able to live, which the mere English hardly do. And yet though we be naturalized by birth or education (which is a second kind of birth), and so consequently joined with them in religion, yet until we plot or effect some notable villainy with them as to help to ruin the next English neighbor and his family, to oppose the government and conclude with the subversions of the state (*quoad posse*), they will never trust us. Which is a maxim that the Ignatian sect do hold with all the English fugitives of any eminence either in birth, courage, or wit, so to engage them that being thereby unfit to return they may find a necessity of dependency upon them.[96]

The Irish were intensely superstitious. Devout Catholics they might be, they had nonetheless kept from pre-Christian times in their western isolation a uniquely rich heritage of magic and luck. The charms and taboos of Irish life were numerous, colorful, and, to the Englishman, largely irrational. Father Good, as an English Catholic cleric, was shocked at their pagan character, but he was sufficiently interested to give a long catalogue of Irish superstitions.[97] Moryson was more entertained than shocked, though he puts on a long face at times.[98] Rich mainly expressed his disgust.[99] Yet together they contrive to show that very many of the characteristic Irish taboos revolved around their animals and reflect the ancient pastoral matrix inside which the Irish lived.

Meredith Hanmer jotted down a few notes which indicate the kind of beliefs and practices associated with cattle. One is worth giving for this reason, even though it is not self-explanatory: "On May Eve they drive their cattle upon their neighbors' corn and eat it up. They are wont to begin from the East. . . . Unless they do so upon May Eve, the witch will have power over the cattle all the year following." [100] Good and Moryson combine to record the following on cows and horses:

> They are much offended if a man commend their cattle, except withal he say "God save them" or else spit upon them.
>
> Their horses shall live long if they give no fire out of the house . . . That some ill-luck will fall to their horses if the rider, having eaten eggs, do not wash his hands after them, or be not careful to choose eggs of equal bigness.[101]

If the rationale of these is not evident, it may be that other superstitions may be more easily penetrated, while their connection with the pastoral heritage is at least suggested.

Moon lore, witches, wise women, fairies, the shades of heroic ancestors, all enter into Father Good's account. Thus, "I cannot tell," he says,

> whether the wilder sort of the Irishry yield divine honor unto the moon, for, when they see her first after the change, commonly they bow the knee and say over the Lord's Prayer and, so soon as they have made an end, they speak unto the moon with a loud voice in this manner: "Leave us as whole and sound as thou hast found us."

Or again:

> They think there be some that bewitch their horses with looking upon them: and then they use the help of some old hags who, saying a few prayers with a loud voice, make them well again.

The fairies were thought to be involved if a mishap took place in an open place:

> When any man hath caught a fall upon the ground, forthwith he starteth up again on his feet and turneth himself round three times toward his right hand. With his sword, skean, or knife he diggeth into the earth and fetcheth up a turf, for that, they say, the earth doth yield a spirit. And if, within some two or three days, he fell sick there is sent a woman skillful in that kind unto the said place

and there she sayeth on this wise: "I call thee P. from the East and West, South and North, from the forests, woods, rivers, meres, the wild wood-fairies, white, red, black, etc." And withal bolteth out certain short prayers. Then returneth she home unto the sick party to see whether it be the disease called "Esane" [but *esláine* is simply sickness], which they are of opinion is sent by the fairies, and whispereth a certain odd prayer, with a *Pater Noster*, into his ear, putteth some coals into a potful of fair water, and so giveth more certain judgment of the disease than many of our physicians can.

He tells us also:

They suppose that the souls of such as are deceased go into the company of certain men, famous in those places, touching whom they retain still fables and songs, as of giants, "Fin-Mac-Huyle" [Fionn mac Cumhaill], "Oscar Mac-Oshin" [Oscar mac Oisín]. And they say that by illusion they oftentimes do see such.[102]

These examples only scratch the surface of the rich vein uncovered by the Elizabethan observers. Though peasant life in any European country is rich in such beliefs and practices, there is no reason to believe that they were not especially luxuriant in Ireland or that they did not seem genuinely strange to English, especially to urban English, observers.

Englishmen were not indifferent to the Irish language. From Andrew Boorde, Catholic priest and physician, who in the 1540's made a list of Irish words with English equivalents,[103] to Meredith Hanmer, a Protestant clergyman, who in the last years of Elizabeth's reign included some Irish verses amongst his antiquarian collections,[104] men were found who did more than scoff at what was spoken by the Irish. Officially, there was strong English disapproval that most of the Old English, even of the Pale, were bilingual and that many of them spoke much more Irish than English. The old urban families, like that of Richard Stanyhurst in Dublin, tried to hold out against this trend, and Richard certainly disapproved of it, yet Edmund

Campion, though he lived with the Stanyhursts while in Ireland, learned enough about the Irish chronicles to have a measure of respect for them,[105] and Spenser, as we saw, had some poems translated so that he could attempt to estimate their value. Most observers on the English side expressed their antagonism to Irish on political grounds: even those who did not profess to do so were influenced by these considerations. Thus Moryson, whose acquaintance with non-English languages was considerable, wrote "touching the Irish language":

It is a peculiar language, not derived from any other radical tongue (that I ever could hear, for myself neither have nor ever sought to have any skill therein). . . . But all I have said hereof might well be spared, as if no other tongue were in the world I think it would never be missed either for pleasure or necessity.[106]

The other side of the picture was that the Irish on their side had as little liking for the use of the English language, though this hostility was probably most marked in the North, since in the South and Midlands, Irish and Old English groups being intermingled, the Irish had become more accustomed to the use of English. An anonymous writer of 1598 is probably thinking mainly of Ulster when he writes: "For language, they do so despise ours as they think themselves the worse when they hear it." [107] Stanyhurst tells us: "One demanded merrily why Oneile that last was [Shane] would not frame himself to speak English? 'What,' quoth the other in a rage, 'thinkest thou that it standeth with Oneile his honor to writhe his mouth in clattering English?' " [108]

The English commentators who denounced the Old English for speaking little or much Irish were inclined to make categorical statements about language in general, such as this of Spenser's: "It is unnatural that any people should love another's language more than their own." [109] They were precisely those who advocated that the Irish should be induced or forced to give up their own language, since, as Moryson put it, "In general all nations have thought of nothing more powerful to unite minds than the community of language." [110]

Against this background some English attitudes betray almost too much simplicity of mind. Thus the writer of a discourse in 1598 complained about the oppositeness of the Irish:

For none, with his goodwill, will be called Henry, Edward, Richard, George, Francis, or suchlike English names, but rather Morrogh, Moriertagh, Tirlogh, and such harsh names, both for a difference to distinguish them from the English, and as a mark of their offspring, which they observe with as great care as they joy therein with great boast.[111]

The more general comments on the Irish tended to stress that they had inherently many good qualities if they could be weaned from their old social system and traditional habits. Father Good says:

And to speak in general of them all, this nation is strong of body and passing nimble: stout and haughty in heart; for wit quick, martial, prodigal, and careless of their lives; enduring travail, cold, and hunger; given to fleshly lust; kind and courteous to strangers; constant in love, in enmity implacable; light of belief, greedy of glory, impatient of abuse and injury; and, as [Gerald of Wales] said in old time, in all affections most vehement and passionate. If they be bad, you shall nowhere meet with worse: if they be good, you can hardly find better.[112]

Stanyhurst is close to this:

The people are thus inclined: religious, frank, amorous, ireful, sufferable of infinite pains, very [vain]glorious, many sorcerers, excellent horsemen, delighted with wars, great almsgivers, passing in hospitality. The lewder sort, both clerks and laymen, are sensual and overloose in living. The same, being virtuously bred up or reformed, are such mirrors of holiness and austerity that other nations retain but a shadow of devotion in comparison of them. . . . Greedy of praise they be and fearful of dishonor.[113]

Another general description was written about 1588. It is Stanyhurst with a hostile bite added to it:

The people are of nature very glorious, frank, ireful, good horsemen, able to endure great pains, delighted in war, [of] great hospitality, of religion (for the most part) papists, great gluttons, and of a sensual and vicious life, deep dissemblers, secret in displeasure, of a cruel, revenging mind and irreconcilable, for when the parties which were at variance are to be joined in secret league of amity, even when they offer one another a drop of their blood and sup it up together before the Bishop, and carry each other upon their back in the church where they use to meet, in doing thereof they practice each other's destruction. Of wit they are quick and capable, kindhearted where they take, and of exceeding love toward their foster brethren. Of complexion they are clear and well favored, both men and women, tall and corpulent bodies, but of themselves careless and bestial.[114]

Looking back over nearly twenty years of interest in Ireland, Sir John Harington in 1605 spoke of Irish and Old English indifferently in a more urbane and tolerant fashion. He said:

Neither is the country without rare examples of fidelity in servants, of love and chastity in matrons, howsoever some pens have taxed the one with treachery, the other with incontinency. Gold hath corrupted of both sorts in all countries, yet have there been many men there that neither for terror or reward would forsake their masters even to the loss of their lives. . . . I never found in the remote shires of England and Wales either the gentry more kind in their fashion or entertainment, or the merchants and townsmen and women more civil in behavior, or the mean sort and peasants more loving and serviceable, where they are honestly used, throughout all the five provinces.[115]

CHAPTER VIII

The Irish Brought to Life

THOUGH Elizabethan English observers provided sufficient information about the clothing of the Irish, they did not, surprisingly, leave us any really adequate original drawings of Irishmen.[1] Our best views of sixteenth-century Irishmen we owe to Continental artists, principally to Albrecht Dürer and to the Flemish painter Lucas de Heere, though we can supplement them from Elizabethan woodcuts.

In 1521 Dürer met a party of Irish soldiers which he sketched (Plate 2). Two were galloglasses, described, as we have seen, by Stanyhurst. Equipped for war, they wore military clothing, but their three attendants have the characteristic Irish dress, wearing over their other clothes "their Irish mantle, or shag rugs with a deep fringed purfle [border] and the same daintily set out with sundry colors," as Father Good describes it,[2] which could be pulled over the head like a hood. Spenser at once eulogized and condemned the Irishman's mantle: "In summer he can wear it loose, in winter he can wrap it close, at all times he can use it, never heavy, never cumbersome," yet it could also mask many dark practices.[3] The men had long tunic-like shirts hanging below the knee. These were, later in the century at least, kilted at the waist ("folded in wrinkles," as Fynes Moryson puts it).[4] "They stain their large wide shirts," Good tells us,

91

"a saffron color . . . with the boughs, bark, and leaves of the poplar tree, . . . adding thereto the rind of the wild arbutus tree, salt, together with saffron," and urine as mordant.[5] The saffron, according to Spenser and Moryson, was "to avoid lousiness, incident to the wearing of foul linen." [6] The Irish, Moryson says, like to use great quantities of cloth, "twenty or thirty ells." [7] With the shirt the men in Dürer's drawings are wearing a short jacket, belted at the waist, and with wide hanging sleeves. They have no trews, the tight Irish trousers. Two of the men have shaggy hair, hanging over their eyes, but there are clear signs that it has been slightly trimmed. They were extremely proud of the "long, crisped bushes of hair which they term glibs, and the same they nourish with all their cunning; to crop the front thereof they take it for a notable piece of villainy," Stanyhurst tells us,[8] so it is clear that the men illustrated here have gone some way to conform with a new environment. Spenser strongly resented their glibs; "hanging down over their eyes and monstrously disguising them, which are both very bad and hurtful." [9] He also called attention to their long mustaches, saying they refused to wear full beards (though old men did so). The Irish poet Laoiseach Mac an Bhaird, apostrophizing the men "who follow English ways, who cut short your curling hair," urges them not to give up their long hair, "the best adornment in all the land of Ireland." [10] In the drawing, the men have mustaches, but they too look as if they had been somewhat trimmed. Leather shoes (brogues) or sandals make up their attire, though two men have bare feet. The galloglasses are covered with long padded surcoats coming down to the calf over their coats of mail; they wear helmets, or leather and metal headpieces, and carry the great two-handed sword, long-handled ax, long dart or short spear, and short bow, all characterized in prose by Spenser in his *View* but also resurrected in the giant Grantorto:

92

The Irish Brought to Life

All armed in a coat of iron plate,
Of great defense to ward the deadly fear,
And on his head a steel cap he did wear
Of color rusty brown but sure and strong;
And in his hand an huge poleax did bear,
Whose steel was iron-studded but not long,
With which he wont to fight, to justify his wrong.[11]

It would appear that late in the reign of Henry VIII an artist of some quality visited Ireland and made figure drawings of both Irish men and women and Old English women, if not men. We do not know who he was, precisely when he came to Ireland, or anything about him except that his drawings remained available in England between Henry VIII's reign, which ended in 1547, until about 1570 at least. An engraving of one of them, apparently made in England, from its inscription "Draun after the quicke," that is from life, is in the Ashmolean Museum at Oxford (Plate 3).[12] It shows a more varied group of Irishmen than Dürer's, apparently this time made up of kern (*ceithearn*), light infantry. They carry short broadswords, with strikingly ornamented hilts and pommels, and long daggers (*sceana*), but their most characteristic weapon, the throwing dart, is not shown. One wears a very shaggy mantle; the lengthy shirts are tucked in at the waist but not pleated and have long flowing sleeves coming away from the elbows. Over them they wear very short jackets, the chests, shoulders, and sleeves of which are elaborately embroidered with appliqué designs, the lower part, barely reaching the waist, being pleated. The sleeves are slit to let the shirt sleeves hang down but can be closed at the wrists with tapes. One man has a leather helmet; none are shod.

Lucas de Heere, an able Flemish artist, was in England between 1569 and 1577, and he has left us four water-color drawings, three now in the University Library at Ghent and one in the British Museum, which include in all seven figures in Irish

93

costume and five women in Old English dress (the three with Irish figures being Plates 4–6).[13] As one of them, the most important for our purpose (Plate 4), is headed *Irlandois et Irlandoise comme ils alloyent accoustres estans seruice de feu Roy Henry,* that is, it shows Irish dress under Henry VIII, and as all of them have stylistic similarities to the woodcut already referred to, it seems highly probable that they derive from the artist whose drawing lies behind the woodcut already described. (The likelihood of the association is best judged by comparing the men in Plate 3 with those in Plate 4.) It does not seem, therefore, that De Heere went to Ireland or drew Irish figures from life. The evidence he himself provides in the Ghent manuscript is ambiguous: "I have added hereafter," he says in the text attached to the album, "the savage and the tame Irishman as they nowadays go about and have gone about in the days of King Henry the Eighth." [14] Since the two drawings in this collection (Plates 4 and 6) are the two which belong without doubt to an earlier generation, we are left with only a single drawing containing a "savage" Irishman, namely that in the British Museum (Plate 5), which is likely to be contemporaneous with the artist, though it is not necessarily so. We know from other work he did while in England that De Heere was a careful copyist, and it is likely that his versions faithfully reflect the originals. Whether the artist he copied was some English member of Holbein's school or a Continental visitor, it is still quite impossible to indicate. We can, however, with fair probability rely on the engraving and the De Heere drawings, together with the Dürer drawing, as providing us with a visual representation of typical Irishmen and Irishwomen of the period between 1520 and, perhaps, 1560.

In one of the drawings (Plate 4) we get the first effective picture of the Irishwoman. She is wearing a mantle of brownish cloth, rather finer in quality than that worn by the men, but without colored, or indeed any prominent, fringes. Good speaks of a "side garment" worn under the mantle.[15] It is not clear whether he means an undergarment (inside garment) or one fastened at the side. In the drawing she has two garments showing under the mantle, a long green one, probably a smock, like the man's shirt, but one loose enough at the top to leave the breasts almost or wholly uncovered. Above it she seems to be wearing a skirt of lighter color. Spenser said of the loose wandering woman that "in summer you shall find her arrayed commonly but in her smock and mantle." [16] In the drawing the woman's golden hair hangs loosely down her shoulders, below a roll of cloth, white, lightly striped with red. John Speed says, "The women wore their hair plaited in [a] curious manner, hanging down their backs and shoulders, from under folded wreaths of fine linen, rolled about their heads," which exactly describes De Heere's subject, but Speed speaks of it "rather loading the wearer than delighting the beholder; for as the one was most seemly, so the other was unsightly." [17] Good says much the same.[18] The style of the linen headdress varied from place to place: Moryson notes one flat on the top and broad at the sides "not much unlike a cheese mot [mold], if it had a hole to put in the head." [19] But he is clearly describing something which covered the whole head. The woman in the drawing has a hat as well as her roll. It seems to be a red cap, attached by a band of cloth coming under the chin, ornamented with pieces of green cloth, caught up from the rim and secured at the top of her head with a metal, perhaps a golden, band. She has none of the many chains, necklaces, and bracelets on which Moryson and Good remarked.[20] She is also barefoot. The woman is pleasant-looking, and Stanyhurst characterizes Irishwomen in general, as we saw, as "well favored, clean-colored, fair-handed," [21] though Moryson adds that "it would turn a man's stomach to see an old woman in the morning before breakfast," having in the house "only . . . their privy parts covered with a rag of linen and their bodies with a loose mantle." [22]

95

The figures of the men in the De Heere drawings are closely similar to those in the engraving already referred to, but the color gives a more vivid impression of their dress, an old man's faded green mantle, the blue of the young man's as he carries it on one shoulder to show off his short red jacket, with its bands of gold embroidery, and the brightness of his yellow shirt. One of the jackets on an older man in the party which contains the woman is embroidered with tendrils of gold and silver flowers on a green cloth. With them is a long-haired boy, in the characteristic shirt but with a tight-sleeved jacket, who is playing the bagpipes, war pipes with long chanters, used to encourage the fighting men.

The men and women in the engraving and in the two main De Heere drawings are well-dressed, serious, dignified, or cheerful figures, but the man shown in the third De Heere drawing (Plate 5), along with an Old English noblewoman, is a less attractive individual. His mantle, worn with the fringe over his head, is old and its fringe tattered, his face looks dirty, and his smile, though ingratiating, has a hint of menace in it also. The pommel of his short sword shows at his waist and reinforces the somewhat sinister character he represents. There seems little doubt that he is intended as one of the "idlemen," an unemployed kern, who was likely to have wandered off on a begging or robbing expedition. This would explain the touch of intimidation he appears to be putting into an attempt to extract alms from the lady. This figure, perhaps, best exemplifies the picture of the Irish mantle as the cloak of a thief which it so often bore in English eyes. Its versatility as a garment was highly regarded when it was thought of as a covering for English soldiers, for whom it was available at five shillings each, but it was praised and condemned in the same breath by several writers before Spenser. Sir William Herbert, a Munster colonial promoter, for example, wrote in 1585 of the mantle serving unto the Irish as to a hedgehog his skin or to a snail her shell for a garment by day and a house by night. It maketh them, with the continual use of it, more apt and able to live and lie out of bogs and woods, where their mantle serveth them for a mattress and a bush for a bedstead, and thereby they are less addicted to a loyal, dutiful, and civil life.[23]

We are in rather a different case when we move away from these few illustrations which have been linked with immediately pre-Elizabethan times to undoubtedly contemporary Elizabethan costume drawings. There are few originals on which we can depend. There is a striking little sketch of Turloch Luineach O Neill by Barnaby Googe,[24] the poet, which is much better than anything amongst the other surviving drawings he made, but this (Frontispiece) shows only the head, and the tallish felt hat O Neill is wearing may not be distinctively Irish in style (though it is not easy to find an English hat precisely similar at this period). There are a number of small sketches of Irishmen, kern, galloglasses, horsemen, and civilian hangers-on of the English and Irish forces in the surviving topographical drawings by the Welsh soldier John Thomas of Belleek in October, 1593 (details in Plates 19–20),[25] and of Enniskillen in February, 1594, and also in a drawing by an unknown artist of the taking of the Earl of Ormond prisoner in 1600 [26] (detail in Plate 21). In these the Irish kern is seen stripped down for action to his brogues, his very tight trews, and a close-fitting jerkin coming only to the waist, topped by a (usually) conical headpiece. He is found as often using a harquebus, the favorite firearm of the period, as bow and arrows or his traditional dart. The galloglass, too, has discarded his long encumbering coat of mail (and surcoat) for a somewhat similar garb to the kern (though he is likely to be wearing at least a metal breastplate), but continues to use as weapons his great sword and his halberd-like ax. Sir Jerome Bowes at the court of Ivan IV in 1583 saw his personal guards "holding upon their shoulders each of them a broad ax, much like to a galloglass ax of Ireland, thin and very sharp, the 'steale' or handle not past a half yard long," [27] though the Irish examples would have longer shafts. The horseman rides on his Irish saddle, "either long, narrow pillions bumbasted or bare boards of that fashion," as Moryson describes them.[28] There is a fuller description by Luke Gernon, not written however before 1620, which is more specific:

The Irish saddle is called a pillion, and it is made on this form. The tree [the basic framework] is as of an ordinary saddle, but the seat is a plain table of two foot long and a foot broad or larger, high mounted and covered with a piece of checkered blanketing [but seen padded at either end in some illustrations]. It is not tied with girths, but it is fastened with a breastplate before and a crupper behind, and a surcingle in the middle [this is normally a girth and he has said there are none: he must mean there is a single girth not two—see Plate 11]. The men ride upon it astride with their legs very far extended and toward the horse neck [and so do not use stirrups]. If the horse be dull, they spurgall him in the shoulder. It seemeth very uneasy to us, but they affirm it to be an easy kind of riding.

Though it takes us from our military picture, we may add his remaining comment: "If it be, it is very useful, for a man may ride astride with a woman behind him aside, and a man may ride with a woman behind him, all upon the like saddle. It is an excellent fashion to steal a wench and to carry her away." [29]

The Irish horse soldier was usually protected by a short coat of mail and a stout helmet of leather or steel or a combination of both, while he held a target (a small shield) and used a long lance as his primary and a short sword as his secondary weapon.

Civilians in these drawings have the brogues and tight trews of the kern, with a short jacket having brief or no sleeves and, sometimes, seemingly, a short tail; the characteristic shirt cannot be distinguished, so that if it was worn beneath the jacket it has shrunk from its former extravagance.

The drawing of the Irish lackey which appears in the album of Hieronymus Tielch [30] (Plate 7), who visited England in the early years of the seventeenth century, was almost certainly made there rather than in Ireland. There is no indication that Tielch did the drawing himself, though he may have done so, but it is most likely that he purchased the album ready-made in London, where the Irish horseboy or personal servant was a familiar sight. The drawing is valuable for its color indications, the tight trews the man is wearing being a pinkish-red and the short jacket a clear bright blue (now somewhat rubbed), while his brogues are of dark leather. His long fair hair does not hang over his eyes in a glib but is parted in the middle to fall down on his shoulders. The long sword under his left arm is possibly supported behind by a belt which holds up his trews. He has a dart, nearly as long as himself and fletched like an arrow, in his left hand. The figure is very similar to those seen in miniature in the drawing of the taking of the Earl of Ormond in 1600 (Plate 21), though here the darts are much longer and look like pikes, while they are not fletched, and to other small figures in the Ballyshannon fight of 1593 (Plate 20).

More valuable in their range, though not, of course, so near their subjects, are the woodcuts, "pictures and 'portractours' [portraits] made by painter's cunning skill, with gestures of the Irish kern set out by quivering quill" in John Derricke's book on Ireland.[31] Made and devised by the author himself in 1578 (though two plates are signed "F.D."), the woodcuts seem reliable on details where they can be compared with other sources and add a good deal of their own, though they are explicitly unfavorable to the Irish throughout. Nothing is known of the author, but a John Derick, gentleman, who was collector of customs at Drogheda [32] may well have been he (a Master Derrick afterward served Sir Robert Sidney in the Low Countries as a surgeon, 1597–1601).[33] They are accompanied by a series of verses, partly narrative, partly descriptive, which are of some documentary value but much less than the engravings.

One special contribution of the Derricke cuts is that they confirm the impression already expressed that there has been some appreciable modification of the Irish shirt in the second half of the century. It has become much shorter and is pleated tightly at the waist so that it falls now only some little way down the thigh, though it retains the flowing sleeves (not perhaps with the same luxuriance). Over it is worn a jacket or jerkin, tight around the body but flared and pleated below the waist. It has either very short sleeves or long sleeves which are slit underneath to allow the shirt sleeves to hang through, as in the earlier pictures (Plates 2–5). The trews, absent in the earlier figures, are now invariable, as are the brogues, no bare feet being shown. Derricke's verses denouncing the kern describe them:

With mantles down unto the shoe, to lap them in by night:
With spears and swords and little darts to shield them from despite.
And let some have their breeches close, to nimble things annexed.[34]

One group provides a strip cartoon. We may introduce it by Derricke's picture of a particularly notorious woodkern (Plate 10), Rory Og O More, shown as a serious elderly man, wrapped in his cloak, who is nonetheless an outlaw who lives by attacking the settled territories. Yet not only the outlaws but the Irish magnates enjoy cattle raiding. We are shown another picture of an Irish lord, very differently dressed (Plate 11). Moryson tells us, "The gentlemen, or lords of countries, wear close breeches and stockings of the same piece of cloth [i.e., trews], of red or such light color, and a loose coat, and a cloak or three-cornered mantle, commonly of coarse light stuff made at home, and their linen is coarse and slovenly." [35] In the engraving the man's jerkin and hat are perhaps more nearly English than Irish in style, but he is otherwise dressed as Fynes Moryson though his clothing is neat as well as of high quality. on the left is handing him a light spear, since we are being shown his preparations for a cattle raid. This kern is wearing the shorter shirt with its elaborately pleated skirt and its wide sleeves, over tight trews—"their said breeches are so close," says Moryson, "as they expose to full view, not only the noble, but also the shameful parts, yea they stuff their shirts about their privy parts, to expose them more to the view" (as did the contemporary English codpiece). A horseboy is holding a short throwing spear in one hand while he restrains the small riding horse, a hobby, for his master.

We are allowed before we go further to see the lord at home (Plate 12). Sir John Harington was to speak enthusiastically of Hugh O Neill's "fern table and fern forms, spread under the stately canopy of heaven." [36] Derricke is somewhat apologetic about his plate, which shows an Ulster lord dining in the open air and mixing ceremony with primitive eating customs. It is worth citing him in detail, as there was clearly a good deal of controversy at the time on just how wild the "wild Irishman" really was:

And if . . . some peradventure (whose judgments are partial in other men's labors) shall cavil at this my imprinted Image or impugn the things therein contained (as reporting matters of untruth), especially the third leaf of this discovered woodkern [the plate in question], affirming no such rudeness in these our days to be practiced with the rudest of that most barbarous nation, to such I reply, . . . saying that it is not our English Pale which in any respect I have touched, nor yet those of the South whom I have impeached, nor yet of the West whom I have nipped, but a people out of the North, whose usages I beheld after the fashion there set down.[37]

These, he goes on to say, are "a people sprung from Macke Swine." He is thus talking of one of the MacSweeney families of

County Donegal, descendents of Argyllshire mercenaries who settled there as hereditary galloglasses after leaving Scotland some two centuries before. They were certainly truly Irish by this time, but they would, as leaders of the fighting aristocracy of the *gallóglaich,* have scorned the name of kern. Derricke's admission must reinforce the point, made elsewhere, that the applicability of many of the most primitive culture traits is more often to Ulster than to the rest of Gaelic Ireland.

The open-air style of living was especially appropriate to the summer encampments,[38] but it was also a matter of principle, with the O Neills at least. Con O Neill, first Earl of Tyrone, for all his promise in 1542 that he would put off Irish ways, is said by an anonymous writer on Ulster of 1598 to have laid down, apparently in 1559, a rigid doctrine of non-assimilation (which Moryson also attributes to his son Shane). We are told:

Upon his deathbed he left his curse to any of his posterity that would either learn English, sow wheat, or make any building in Ulster, saying that language bred conversation [that is, living amongst one another] and consequently their confusion, that wheat gave sustenance with like effect, and, in building, they should do but as the crow doth, make her nest to be beaten out by the hawk.[39]

A calf is being killed at one side of the picture. It is then shown, a little further toward the center, being stewed in a vessel improvised (probably) from its own skin and slung across a slow fire, an exhibition of archaic practice which the Englishman found especially strange. Andrew Boorde, a generation before, made his Irishman say:

> I do use no pot to seethe my meat in,
> Wherefore I do boil it in a beast's skin.
> Then after my meat the broth I do drink up.[40]

Or, as he puts it in his prose description, in a form which suggests he may himself have watched it: "And they will seethe

102

their meat in a beast's skin. And the skin shall be set on many stakes of wood, and then they will put in the water and the flesh. And then they will make a great fire under the skin, betwixt the stakes, and the skin will not greatly burn." [41] Returning to Derricke's picture, we see the friar blessing the board, a cloth draped over a somewhat raised plank (it would seem), on one side of which the diners are seated on cushionlike seats. Of these Derricke says:

> Their cushions are of straw, of rushes, or of hay,
> Made bank-set-wise with withies, their tails to underlay.

Before them are three large dishes—Derricke says:

> Their platters are of wood by cunning turners made.[42]

A single (common?) tankard is all the remaining tableware, the lord cutting the meat with, it seems, his short sword or long skean, on which Derricke comments:

> Long stabbers pluck they forth, instead of handsome knives,
> And with the same they flash me out, good God! what pretty shives.
> Not shives of bread, I mean, for that were very rare,
> But gobs of flesh, not boiled enough, which is their common fare.[43]

The lord's wife sits wrapped in her mantle, with her rolled hair much in evidence; the friars are also mantled, but the lord has a short jacket only. A bard, dressed like a kern, is reciting or singing a eulogy to the lord and is being accompanied by a harper.

Derricke's verses are not elegant, but they convey his attitude effectively enough:

> Now when their guts be full, then comes the pastime in.
> The bard and harper melody unto them do begin.
> This bard he doth report the noble conquests done,
> And eke in rhymes shows forth at large their glory thereby won.
> Thus he at random runneth; he pricks the rebels on,
> And shows by such external deeds their honor lies upon.

And more to stir them up, to prosecute their ill,
What great renown their fathers got they show by rhyming skill.
And they most gladsome are to hear of parents' name,
As how by spoiling honest men they won such endless fame.[44]

The attendants are wearing the short kilted shirts and brogues.
At the right-hand side several men are relieving themselves.
This picture is mainly intended as a satire on Irish residual primitiveness, but it also gives, when purged of this intention, some
graphic indication of the simple traditional life of the pastoral
aristocracy.

Our strip cartoon continues with a cattle raid (Plate 13). The
kern march in on an Irish farm led by their piper. Some of them
set fire to the house but do not attempt to harm the occupants;
others drive off the cattle. In a raid of this kind between one
Irish group and another, violence would not usually be done. It
was different when an Old English or planter settlement was
raided. We are shown a sequence in a raid on such a village
(Plate 14). The Irish lord is being blessed by the friar. He leads
his men in to round up the cattle. He is counterattacked by English soldiers and is driven off, the lord being wounded, while
other Irishmen, over whom the friar laments, are killed. Raids
lead to reprisals. We next see (Plate 15) an English attack on the
Irish and the seizure (or recovery) of the cattle. The soldiers kill
any Irishmen they find. One carries a bleeding head as a trophy.
One of the kern is led off prisoner with a halter round his neck.

Like all propaganda, these pictures oversimplify a complex
situation, but they indicate clearly enough what the dreary
round of petty war looked like. They help us to understand the
situation on the borders between the English and the Irish
areas, even if the Irish were not the carnivorous monsters described in Derricke's verse nor, quite, the too savage soldiers
seen in his pictures.

A number of Irish garments have been preserved in peat bogs
and marshes, though, even with modern techniques, dating

them is often very difficult. In 1956 a number of garments were found at Dungiven, County Londonderry, which, after exhaustive investigation, appear likely to be those of one of Hugh O Neill's soldiers in the Elizabethan wars.[45] Brogues, tight trews (here probably of Scottish origin), a skillfully tailored, short-skirted jacket—not at all unlike several shown by Derricke—and a semicircular woolen mantle appear once to have clothed an Irish kern, possibly even one of the O Cahans our Bohemian baron saw in 1599. So, slowly, by search for contemporary representations and by the discovery of their garments, Irishmen and Irishwomen are being brought to life more nearly as the Elizabethan Englishman saw them.

CHAPTER IX

Ireland and America Intertwined

IT IS scarcely surprising that English explorers and colonizers overseas turned to the "wild Irish" as a standard for comparison with foreign cultures. Ireland in a real sense turned English minds toward America.[1] Before the Elizabethans settled down to conquer Ireland there had been little thought of taking up great holdings of land across the Atlantic Ocean, though a few Englishmen had already glanced at the wide open shorelines of North America. But intermittently from about 1520 onward, and less intermittently from the middle of the century, colonization of Ireland by new English settlers had been considered as one way, possibly the best one, of solving for good and all the problem of ruling the Irish. Although two new counties, King's County and Queen's County, had been mapped out in Queen Mary's reign as places for settling English colonists who would defend the Pale from Irish attacks, the colony for some years consisted merely of a few forts in the wilderness. It was not until Sir Henry Sidney came to Ireland in 1566 that these settlements became of any importance. Sidney was familiar with Spanish views on colonial settlement, and it may have been this which made him enlarge the scope of English colonization plans. Shane O Neill, who had established himself in Ulster as ruler of his family's principality, had failed to remain placid after his

submission to Queen Elizabeth in 1562 and had engaged substantial English forces in the north of Ireland, which Sidney led
to victory in 1566. At that point the Lord Deputy had to decide
what should be done with the O Neill lands. He concluded that
an attempt should be made to parcel them out amongst enter-
prising English colonists.[2] They would, like the early Spanish
conquistadores, or for that matter the much earlier Norman in-
vaders of Ireland, be responsible for carving out estates for
themselves with only a minimum of government licensing and
assistance. As his messenger to put these plans before the Queen
in November, 1566, Sidney chose Captain Humphrey Gilbert,
who may have had some part in working out the scheme.[3] Gilbert had already turned his attention to western waters, but in
terms of a Northwest Passage to Cathay on which he had completed a discourse some months earlier. In it English colonies
had figured only as supply stations along the route to Asia. But
in Ireland Gilbert was bitten by the idea that what English gentlemen really needed, especially younger sons of landed gentlemen like himself, who could not hope to inherit paternal lands,
was the prospect of unlimited estates to be won and held in Ireland. The conversion of Queen Elizabeth to the idea of a free-
for-all in the land of her Irish subjects was not achieved easily or
completely. There were many arguments to be urged against the
policy advocated by Sidney and Gilbert, not the least of which
was that it would render any real reconciliation between Irish
and English in the long run impracticable. The Queen did au-
thorize a few enterprises in eastern Ulster, where she was convinced that royal title to the land concerned was at least as good
as that of the Irish occupants, and where, in any event, maraud-
ing and settling Scots from the Western Highlands constituted a
special local problem, justifying, it was thought, colonial experi-
ments. One of these, launched with much publicity in 1571, was
for the planning of an English colony around the great city of
Elizabetha, to be built in the Ards, in County Down. There, like

a Roman municipality on the wilder limits of the Empire, civilization, its backers claimed, might be brought to a savage Irish region. This Utopian dream was that of Sir Thomas Smith,[4] an authority on ancient Rome as well as one of Queen Elizabeth's counselors, and his son Thomas. In practice, the venture aimed at establishing, as the Spanish conquest of Mexico and Peru had done, a colonial aristocracy. The status of the Irish under such a regime was frankly stated by the promoters:

Every Irishman shall be forbidden to wear English apparel or weapon upon pain of death. That no Irishman, born of Irish race and brought up Irish, shall purchase land, bear office, be chosen of any jury or admitted witness in any real or personal action, nor be bound apprentice to any science or art that may endamage the Queen's Majesty's subjects hereafter. . . .

All Irishmen, especially native in that country, which commonly be called churls, that will plow the ground and bear no kind of weapon nor armor, shall be gently entertained, and for their plowing and labor shall be well rewarded with great provision. That no injury be offered to them, and without any coyne, livery, or any other exaction.[5]

This policy thus aimed to eliminate completely the aristocratic and learned classes in Irish society—they were not even, as in earlier plans, to be given the chance of dressing and becoming like Englishmen—and was combined with an encouraging labor policy toward the depressed Irish working peasantry.

The attempt in 1572–1573 to carry out this ambitious plan was on a small and ineffective scale: the killing of Thomas Smith by his Irish servants in 1573 may have stressed the dangers rather than the advantages of such a policy toward the Irish as he envisaged, and it was, for a time, abandoned. Sir Thomas Smith had had some misgivings about the scheme and wrote to the Lord Deputy, Sir William Fitzwilliam, in April, 1573, that he hoped it would not turn out like Thomas Stukely's adventure in 1563, when money—including, we may suspect, some from Sir Thomas—and men were collected for a settlement in Florida but used instead for a sordid piratical cruise in European waters. Smith's words about his son were, unwittingly, prophetic: "I had rather he should adventure his life than that we both should be accounted deceivers of men and enterprisers of Stewelie's voyage of Terra Florida, or a lottery, as some evil tongues did term it." [6]

A few years before, Sir Warham St. Leger, an official serving in Ireland, and a young Cornish squire, Richard Grenville, had taken leases of land around Cork Harbour from the Earl of Desmond at a time when this nobleman was trying to win favor from the English government. During 1568 and 1569 they brought over their families and some tenants,[7] but in July, 1569, there was a sudden rising of many of the Old English and the Irish of Munster under James Fitzmaurice Fitzgerald, a cousin of the Earl (who was at that time detained in England). Soon St. Leger's castles at Kerrycurrihy and Carrigaline had been stormed and Grenville's household at Tracton Abbey—he himself being absent—was overwhelmed, with the loss of seventeen persons. This adverse experiment in colonizing did not, however, discourage Grenville in the longer run from further attempts. Humphrey Gilbert, too, having failed to win full support for a colonizing program in Ulster, appeared in Munster as a military commander and played an important and ruthless part in the suppression of the rising.[8] From 1569 to 1573 he planned, unavailingly, to settle large numbers of Englishmen from the southwestern counties of England in various parts of Munster, but he did not achieve success, because Queen Elizabeth and her advisers thought it unwise to disturb the provincial land settlement, which was, in any event, mainly on feudal lines and under the control of Old English landowners. It was frustration in his Munster plans which turned Gilbert's attention to America, first to renewed speculation about a Northwest Passage and then to plans for exploiting American land.

As Scottish raids on and settlements in County Antrim, in the northeast corner of Ireland, had given cause for anxiety for some years, this area was thought especially desirable as a place to plant settlers. Amongst those who had proposals for doing so was Sir Thomas Gerrard, a prominent Lancashire Catholic landowner. His plans to bring men from Yorkshire, Lancashire, and Cheshire to settle Antrim were seriously considered in 1569–1570 [9] but were eventually rejected, perhaps because it was suspected that Gerrard's religion might render him unreliable in time of emergency.

Walter Devereux, Earl of Essex, was, in 1573, entrusted with the task of planting Antrim and found the Queen herself willing to contribute. Antrim was divided on paper amongst certain English gentlemen, and in 1573 a great expedition set out to occupy and settle it.[10] The venture was almost a complete fiasco: no enemy could be found to fight, Irish and Scots alike having taken themselves into hiding; stores were quite inadequate; and, in any event, large parts of County Antrim looked bleak and uninviting when seen at first hand. As a result, the greater number of the settlers returned rapidly to England. Not so Essex. For some years he attempted to continue the scheme on a smaller scale, in the end with no success. Several Englishmen afterward prominently engaged in American enterprises played some part in the venture. Henry Knollys, son of the Queen's Vice-Chamberlain, Sir Francis Knollys, arrived in 1573 but soon deserted Essex for the delights of piracy in European waters,[11] before making a half-hearted attempt to participate in Humphrey Gilbert's American voyage in 1578. Francis Drake, in the intervals of his piratical raids on the Spaniards in the Caribbean, found time to aid Essex in a raid on Rathlin Island in July, 1575, when, as captain of the Queen's ship "Falcon," he had a hand in killing off the Scottish population, before returning to England to fetch Sir Henry Sidney to Ireland in September in his own bark the "Frigacie." [12] Other well-known overseas venturers were engaged in Ireland in these years. Ralph Lane was one of the purchasers of Sir Henry Sidney's ship, the "Carick Sidney," in 1570,[13] though it is not known whether or not he employed her in the Ulster ventures of Smith and Essex in the years following. Martin Frobisher was reported early in 1573 to be active on the Irish coast, trading in Munster in goods obtained by piracy.[14] Again it is not clear whether he too was engaged in the Ulster ventures, though probably he was not. When Frobisher appears again in Ireland, it is as commander of the Queen's ship "Foresight" in 1580, when he took part in the siege and subsequent massacre at Smerwick.

Sir Humphrey Gilbert—he had been knighted for his military services in Munster—meanwhile meditated the problems of colonization. If Ireland had a social fabric into which it was difficult or impolitic to introduce colonies, might not North America be carved up for this purpose? Thus, in 1578, he obtained from Queen Elizabeth the famous patent which authorized him to conquer and occupy with Englishmen such waste lands as he might find overseas (in North America, although this is not specified), no thought being given to the rights of the non-Christian native inhabitants, who, more savage even than the Irish, were thought not to be of any account. Amongst his associates in his first voyage was Henry Knollys, who proved no more faithful to him than he had been to Essex, deserting as soon as the squadron was at sea to engage in open piracy. The expedition was intended, most probably, for what are now the Carolinas and Virginia, but Gilbert himself was driven back to Ireland and only the "Falcon" under his young half brother, Walter Raleigh, got so far south as the tropics—whether she reached the West Indies we cannot be sure—before returning to England.[15]

Gilbert was able in 1579 to earn money to pay his crews by taking some ships to guard the southern Irish shores against Fitzmaurice's return to start a new rebellion in Munster. He failed to intercept Fitzmaurice and, with Desmond joining in the revolt, a new round of war and desolation began. Walter Raleigh, as captain of a company of infantry, was active in the suppression of the rising. He came back to England in 1581, having marked out some lands in Munster he would like to have, confident of his ability to prescribe for Irish ills. His policy statement on Ireland in 1582 was not extreme: he preferred an attempt to get the cooperation of the lesser landholders, Old English and Irish, to an all-out plantation scheme such as other men were already contemplating.[16] It was, in the end, plantation which was decided on, and Raleigh and Grenville were to be among the beneficiaries of this policy.

Back in England, Raleigh had found Gilbert immersed in a bigger and better American land scheme. He had now turned his attention further north along the eastern shores of North America to Norumbega, the later New England. He had begun cooperation with a group of Catholic gentlemen, headed by Sir George Peckham and the Sir Thomas Gerrard who had previously been interested in Antrim. With them were associated Sir William Stanley, who had had a long career as a soldier in Ireland and who eventually was to desert to the Spaniards at Deventer; Richard Bingham, who was to have a prominent military career in Ireland from 1586 onward; and Martin Frobisher, who was slowly recovering from the collapse in 1578 of his Northwest Passage venture. Interested, too, was Sir Philip Sidney, who had, as we have seen, prescribed for Ireland's reform after a brief visit in 1576.[17] The Catholics wished to acquire American land which would be free of the heavy burdens laid on their English estates; but many were soon scared away by Spanish threats that they would get their throats cut in North America, the whole of which the Spaniards claimed for themselves. When some millions of acres of land had been disposed of on paper, Gilbert set sail himself in June, 1583. Raleigh, now something of a favorite at court, was not himself able to go and was forced to put his "Bark Raleigh" under the command of Michael Butler, who had been his lieutenant in the Irish wars; but the ship turned back ignominiously, while Gilbert, after formally annexing Newfoundland, was lost on his way home.[18]

After Gilbert's death, Peckham tried for a time to keep the Catholic project afloat, but, as Gerrard and others had retired from it, soon gave up, leaving Rhode Island and Connecticut to be settled by English Puritans of a later generation. Christopher Carleill, Sir Francis Walsingham's stepson, whose objective seems to have been Maine or Nova Scotia, did set out in the summer of 1584 but broke up his expedition in Ireland and settled down to establish a small fort and settlement in Coleraine, on the northeastern border of the O Neill territory in Ulster.[19]

John Rastell in 1517, Thomas Stukely in 1563, and Christopher Carleill in 1584 all carried intending settlers of North America only so far as Ireland, where they broke off their voyages, but only in the last case were the colonists absorbed into Irish plantations instead of being brought to found new ones, in virgin soil, farther to the west. Carleill remained in Ireland for some years, taking time off to go with Drake to the West Indies and visiting the English colony at Roanoke Island in 1586. After 1590 he revived notions of an American settlement, which he did not live to attempt, as he is said to have died in 1593.[20]

The real heir to Gilbert's plans was Sir Walter Raleigh. He took over Gilbert's patent in 1584 and sent out a reconnaissance expedition; one of the ships was under the command of another of his associates in the Irish wars, Arthur Barlowe. Raleigh aimed at lower latitudes and received a good account from his agents of what is now the North Carolina coast: Queen Elizabeth allowed it to be called Virginia, and Sir Richard Grenville was charged with carrying to it in 1585 the first soldier-settlers, who were to explore the land and make it an effective English base against Spain. To command those who stayed behind, Ralph Lane had been sent for: a soldier engaged in mopping-up operations after the Desmond wars in County Kerry, he had also begun to carve himself an estate there, but he agreed to act as colonel and governor of the shore party in the Virginian venture, bringing his Irish boy with him (compare Plate 19) who was after to help him bring down his biggest American game, the Indian chieftain Pemisapan.[21]

How valuable Lane's Irish experience was to him in the American wilds we cannot say; he did his job well and survived the winter. It was not his fault that Grenville did not arrive in time with supplies and that he had to leave Virginia with Drake in June, 1586. Grenville and Raleigh, too, had been preoccupied to some extent with Ireland over the winter of 1585–1586, as, at last, a plan to split up the greater part of Munster into estates for English colonists had been agreed, and both these gentlemen were applicants for Irish land. Eventually they emerged as owners of great seignories. Grenville revived his old partnership with St. Leger and took over again lands from which they had been expelled in 1569.[22] Raleigh was granted a great block of land in eastern County Cork and County Waterford amounting to some 40,000 acres and centering round Lismore Castle and the old town of Youghal. If Grenville was late at Roanoke Island in 1586, then Ireland may have had something to do with it. His leaving only a small party behind, which was eventually chased away by the local Indians, broke the continuity in colony-building. John White, the topographical artist in the first settlement, brought out a fresh colony from England in 1587, but two Irishmen amongst the settlers (they may have been rather casually recruited) deserted in the West Indies.[23] One of them, Darby Glavin (or Glande), turned up many years later as a soldier in the Spanish garrison of St. Augustine, Florida; Dennis Carroll, the other, disappeared. But White had to desert his settlers on Roanoke Island to go home for more supplies and, although he did not know it, left them for good. Grenville was unable to convoy him to America in 1588, as his ships were needed for naval tasks and he, indeed, spent part of that fateful year on Irish service, while White struggled unavailingly to get to America, succeeding in the end only in 1590, when he found the colony had gone from Roanoke Island, no one knew where.

The Munster settlement was planned very much as Sir Humphrey Gilbert had thought of his Norumbega dominion in 1582–1583, with great estates to be cut up and handed over for liberal rents to "undertakers" who promised to install specified numbers of English tenants and to expel all native Irish. By 1589 the Grenville estate had on it 108 men and Raleigh's larger lordship 144 men, 73 of them having their families with them.[24] These numbers were much less than their full quotas, under the official scheme, but they show how plantation in Ireland could rapidly become a substantial movement. There were at least 1,000 New English settlers in all in Munster by 1589 and some hundreds of women and children as well. Many Irish laborers were taken on to till the wasted land and a number of holdings were illegally let to Irishmen. Although much of the area covered by the plantation had been in Old English rather than in Irish ownership, the planting of Englishmen there seemed a threat to the rest of Ireland, where Gaelic life still in a manner flourished.

In 1589 Thomas Hariot was one of Raleigh's tenants at Molana Abbey on his Munster estate.[25] He had been the scientific recorder of the 1585 Virginia colony and had been, as he said himself, in his tract on the voyage, "in dealing with the natural inhabitants specially employed." Now, after his pioneer ethnological work amongst the Carolina Algonkian Indians,[26] he had come to settle among the Irish. Four years later we find John White also reappearing, after giving up his Virginia colony for lost, as a planter in Munster, since in 1593 he wrote to Richard Hakluyt from Newtown in the Great Wood of Kilmore, not far from the modern town of Charleville (Rath Luirc) in County Cork, where he had settled on the estate of Hugh Cuffe.[27] From drawing Indians to go with Hariot's descriptions of them, he too had come to live in Ireland, though we do not know that he drew any pictures of the Irish. It is almost certain, also, that other short-term Virginia settlers who had served with Lane returned to Ireland and some of them to Munster. Lane himself re-entered the Irish service when he was made mustermaster of the army there in 1592, being knighted for his services the following year and spending the last ten years of his life on military affairs in Ireland.

The Munster plantation was not yet on a permanent footing. War had gradually developed between the Queen's forces and the Irish lords of Ulster in the early 1590's, and in 1598 the fire caught hold of Munster. Irish laborers and tenants, with some Irish and Old English landowners who had retained their lands, rose against the English settlements in October, and before even slight attack the colony crumbled. A caustic chronicler tells us:

All the English of the seignory of Sir Walter Raleigh . . . ran away. The inhabitants . . . of the seignory of Sir Warham Sentleger took their flight. . . .

The misery of the Englishry was great. The wealthier sort, leaving their castles and dwelling-houses, and their victual and furniture, made haste into walled towns, where there was no enemy within ten miles. The meaner sort (the rebellion having overtaken them), were slain, man, woman and child; and such as escaped came all naked to the towns.[28]

This cataclysm was for the Munster colony the equivalent of the 1622 Indian massacre in Virginia. It shook the settlement to the core; it also led on to a still sterner policy toward the native inhabitants. But in Munster there were the walled port towns like Cork and Kinsale to which settlers could escape, and there was refuge in nearby England to be found by sea. An English army, too, was soon to wipe Irishmen, combatants and non-combatants alike, off the Munster lands. By 1603 the settlers could, if they wished, come back.

Ireland and America Intertwined

The Spaniards were seen by some English propagandists as valuing Ireland, potentially, even more highly than their own overseas colonies. The anonymous author of a polemical tract has a passage to this effect:

Why do they of the Spanish faction . . . give it out . . . that they will never come to any agreement, peace, and concord until they hear an end of the Irish wars? . . . They quarter and brave it out everywhere (but especially beyond the seas) with the great hopes they have of making England a Japonian Island [an island as isolated, that is, as Japan was thought to be from China] by conquest of Ireland, according to the old prophecy "He that England will win, through Ireland he must come in." What, man, Ireland? Yea, I say Ireland. What, Ireland won from Her Majesty? Yea, and from Teron [Tyrone] too! Tush man, it is a jest.[29]

Inflated as this may seem, Spanish aims were seen in Ireland as the converse of English ones, colonial in each case, but with strong strategic overtones. Indeed, against this view of Spanish hopes and fears, Englishmen began to think of Ireland as in a real sense alternative to colonial settlements in America, though there remained the problem of how to dispose of the Irish. A writer in 1603 said: "Truly I have heard that the Spaniards and others have reported a long time since that, if the princes of England knew what a jewel Ireland were, they needed not to seek the discovery of foreign countries to inhabit in." [30]

In the very last years of Queen Elizabeth's reign the air was full of fresh schemes for settling Ireland and America with Englishmen. The disasters in Virginia and in Munster were making prophets cautious; experience was giving rise to some study of the comparative problems of colonization. The largest problem was how, in lands where there was no gold or silver to be found or tropical riches to be exploited in crops or timber, the initial capital could be found for colonial experiment. One anonymous English theorist, discussing the possibilities of English settlement in the St. Lawrence valley about 1600, made these remarks:

The country [the St. Lawrence basin] seems . . . to be cold and to bring forth commodities as cold countries doth, with industry. Our country people, having ever been bred with plenty in a more temperate air and naturally not very industrious at home, [are] less to seek out places where their labors are present and their hopes a little deferred. Whereof we have too good experience by Ireland which [is] near us, a temperate and fertile country, subject to our own laws and half civil, the ports and many towns friendly inhabited. Notwithstanding, many of good reputation [who] become undertakers there in time of peace, could not invite our people, neither in any competent numbers nor constantly in their action, the reason being chiefly that in climates that bring forth but yearly riches, and that with labor, a stock and industry must be ventured upon expectation. Our able men are in the same trade at home already and love ease and security; and [the] poor man wants wealth to disburse anything, wants wisdom to foresee the good, and wants virtue to have patience and constantly attend the reward of . . . good work and industry.[31]

With such a clear-sighted appreciation of the capitalist virtues, English success in colonization could not be long deferred, whether it was in Munster or in Virginia. Renewed plans there were in plenty. In 1602–1603 Sir Walter Raleigh was reviving his quest for a suitable site for a new Virginian colony, while Gosnold, Pring, and others were investigating Gilbert's old hunting ground, Norumbega. In Ireland there were projects without end for renewing the Munster plantation; for taking over piecemeal the whole of the north of Ireland when O Neill was finally defeated (Ralph Lane's last known scheme was one for securing Strangford Lough in County Down, where he had settled, by a colony of "men of trade of Manchester, Liverpool, and Lancashire"[32]); for expelling the Irish entirely from Ireland. Lord Mountjoy favored a cautious approach, with careful selection of colonists, having, too, American conditions in mind as a warning:

Because the Irish and English-Irish were obstinate in Popish super-stition, great care was thought fit to be taken that these new colonies should consist of such men as were most unlike to fall to the barba-rous customs of the Irish, or the Popish superstition of Irish and English-Irish, so as no less cautions were to be observed for uniting them and keeping them from mixing with other than if these new colonies were to be led to inhabit among the barbarous Indians.[33]

On this he must have had discussions with Lane or some other veterans of the Roanoke colony and found they held the view that stricter segregation of English settlers from the local In-dians might have preserved the former.

Mountjoy and others had one specific problem at the end of the wars. How could all the galloglasses and kern mobilized on both sides be settled in a civil society? All were agreed the Irish must be disarmed, but their fighting men could and would do nothing but fight. In 1598, the English Privy Council, when formally asked if it would employ any native Irish troops in the Low Countries or France, had replied, "We see not any oppor-tunity how to effect the same." [34] Hugh Cuffe, who had been John White's landlord when he lived at Newtown, revived the matter in 1600, saying, "I could wish that as soon as conven-iently it may be, that by little and little, their swordsmen should be drawn away to be employed in Her Majesty's foreign wars." [35] This prescription was still perhaps thought a little risky, and in 1601 Mountjoy was hoping that Irish soldiers might be drawn away to still more distant fields, to the Indies no less, where many of them might die off. He told the Privy Council:

I find the Irishry at this time much to affect some journey into the Low Countries, or to the Indies, or to be led to any other place of service. Unto which if it be objected that they will return more able soldiers and more dangerously affected, I can assure your Lordships there is no experience can better the knowledge they have already attained unto, both for the use of their weapons, and taking the advantage of such ground wherein they fight; and it hath been ever seen that more than three parts of four of these countrymen never return, being once engaged in any such voyage.[36]

The proposal was not followed up substantially, though many Irishmen drifted off to join Continental armies, but it revived in 1607, when the Irish kern were showing, still, how unadaptable they were to a peaceful life. In December, 1607, we are told:

In Ireland there are certain kind of swordsmen called kern, descended from horseboys, idle persons, and unlawful propagation. They are base, apt to follow factions and live always by their spoil, and will never be brought to other conformity there. But if they might be drawn from thence and employed to the planting of Virginia, the country should be well freed and time elsewhere eat them out or amend them.[37]

The Spanish ambassador, indeed, reported in January, 1609, that 500 Irishmen were to be sent with an English force to Virginia to fortify it against a possible Spanish attack.[38] Such projects remained concepts only, though in the longer run transportation to English possessions overseas was to be the lot of many recalcitrant Irishmen.

In the early years of the new century plans for large-scale English colonization of Ireland were to some extent in competition with projects to settle Englishmen in America. Sir Arthur Chichester, the Lord Deputy, writing to Lord Salisbury in 1605, had no doubts where King James's duty, honor, and profit lay: the King, he said, would gain more from settling Ireland than from conquering France.[39] He knew of many who endeavored the finding out of Virginia, Guiana, and other remote and unknown countries, and who would leave Ireland waste and desolate, but he regarded their views as exhibiting either absurd folly or willful ignorance. Yet it proved possible within only two or three years to mobilize enough merchant capital and a sufficient number of restless gentry to enable England to embark almost simultaneously on the colonization of Virginia and of Ulster and to carry out both plantations in double harness. That the two ventures were closely associated in men's minds and regarded as identical in character is clear from the correspondence of the day. On March 8, 1610, we hear: "It is hoped the plantation of Ireland may shortly be settled. The Lord Delaware is preparing to depart for the plantation of Virginia," [40] and in December following it is said that, if Spain were diverted by political entanglements with Barbary, "we are more secure for our plantations in Ireland and Virginia." [41] Colonies in Virginia, Bermuda, Newfoundland, and Londonderry provided four out of seven items in a newsletter of June 29, 1611.[42] Already, by 1613, one of the new English settlements in Ulster (in County Cavan) had been christened Virginia after the American colony.[43] Bacon, indeed, did not regard the two plantations as strictly comparable, the Ulster settlement being in his eyes much the more important venture. He said that Virginia differs "as much from this, as Amadis de Gaul differs from Caesar's 'Commentaries.'" [44] King James, naturally, did not look at any part of the island of Great Britain in a colonial light, but in his eyes the new capital of Jamestown and the older capital of Dublin had a very similar colonial character. Each was a door through which English and Scottish colonists could enter, and thereafter the old inhabitants, whether they were Irishmen or Powhatan Indians, would take second place to the imperial colonists.

There was now a new sense of geographical contiguity between the western island and the lands of America. To Bacon in 1621 Ireland was still attached to the Old World—"the second island of the ocean Atlantic." [45] But Richard Whitbourne in 1622 said of Newfoundland that it "lieth near the course and half the way between Ireland and Virginia," [46] while Fynes Moryson, beginning his geographical description of Ireland, gave it a totally new dimension as: "This famous Island in the Virginian Sea." [47]

CHAPTER X

Horror Story

APART from English habits of landholding and administration, two principles of Tudor policy, ingrained in most of the English soldiers and administrators who came to Ireland, worked against the old Irish society. One, already remarked on, was the elimination so far as possible of the unattached man, the rootless one, the vagabond. He was to be driven off the roads, tied down to his village of origin, beaten, deported, enslaved, or even, if he offered open threats to established society, killed off ruthlessly by martial law. The second was closely linked with the first: the uncompromising suppression of rebellion by the slaughter of a substantial proportion of the participants. These two policies were to give Tudor society in England much of its essential character—the pressures for conformity, the petty tyrannies of the landowners as the instruments of "order." They are evidence of the strong authoritarian streak running through Tudor government which may justify to some extent modern descriptions of Tudor rule as despotism, even if Tudor sovereigns were not in any formal sense despots. Each was kept in mind by most English administrators in Ireland.

"Poor Ireland, worse and worse," wrote George Dowdall, Archbishop of Armagh, himself a member of a prominent Old English family, in July, 1558,[1] thus providing an epigraph for a disturbed and unhappy period in Irish history in which conquest was eventually brought about by a series of tragic and devastating wars. At the same time we must be on our guard against taking too black or, of course, too white a view of life in Elizabethan Ireland. If there was much warfare, yet the picture of continuing disorder at almost all times and places which one might gather from following the documents in the State Papers literally is, at least in part, misleading. On the one hand, much of the unsettlement was purely local in its range and minor in character. For substantial periods Irish and Old English districts might be quiet and peaceful, carrying on their traditional ways of life. On the other hand, the continual criticisms of Irish political and social customs, and demands by English officials for their replacement on the grounds that there could otherwise be no peace in the island, were to some extent artificial, representing the point of view of those who wanted to change or destroy Gaelic society in the interests of ease of government from England, the raising of Irish life to what appeared desirable English standards, and the intrusion into Ireland of expropriating English settlers.

Prescriptions for dealing with the anomalies of Irish society varied from the mild-sounding advocacy of close treaty relations with the Irish princes, in which dependence was not to be very much more than nominal provided some measure of stability was attained, to the total extirpation of the Irish people or their wholesale transportation to servitude in England. Hopes of a settlement on a mild basis which would involve the retention of Irish society in some degree of distinctness were maintained, for example, by Sir James Croft,[2] Lord Deputy for a time under Edward VI and for more than a generation a figure at Queen Elizabeth's court. Lord Burghley, after a long flirtation with the policy of inserting local colonies of Englishmen into various parts of Ireland, came round in February, 1575, to this moderate view:

Horror Story

The best is to seek the reformation of Ireland as well by force as by order of justice, [so] that the English may obey laws and the Irishry be kept from rebellion. And so by success of time the Irish to be brought to be governed either by the law of England or by some constitutions to be compounded partly of their own customs and Brehon laws, that are agreeable to reason, and partly of the English laws.[3]

This, from Queen Elizabeth's lord treasurer and her most experienced Irish minister, was not at all an extreme policy, in that it recognized the possibility of a bridge being built between the two legal systems of Ireland and so between the two major societies of the British Isles. Nevertheless, neither Burghley nor his agents were ever able to put across any very coherent set of practical proposals for the attainment of these ends. Burghley's eldest son, Sir Thomas Cecil, writing to the Queen in 1580 in favor of some such liberal policy—one more tolerant than his father had sketched—put his finger on a real obstacle to any permanent accommodation between England and the Irish: lack of trust by the latter in English sincerity. He thought it was quite possible to permit the Irish lords "to continue their ancient greatness, strength, honor, and surety," but, to do so with any hope of success and permanency, it was necessary "to take away the fear of conquest of late deeply seated in the hearts of the wild Irish," and, just as important, "to wink at certain private disorders which do not properly offend the Crown and have by custom long been used in that realm."[4] Such views as those of Burghley would have received little support in practice from either Old English or English officials in Ireland: those of his son would have been derided as hopelessly unrealistic by almost all of them. In practice, English rule, if by no means consistently so, was much harsher than these suggestions might indicate.

The resident officials in Ireland gave considerable thought to the wiping out of two significant and overlapping elements in Irish society, the traveling craftsmen, messengers, and entertain-

ers and the learned class of brehons and poets (there is no specific suggestion for eliminating the physicians). This would have
torn asunder significant parts of the structure of Irish society,
more particularly by eliminating the jurists—the poets were
more difficult to silence. Nor was this only talk: we have already
seen the Earl of Desmond undertake in 1564 to deal with the
poets and gamblers while at the same time he undertook to get
rid of the brehons in territories he commanded. When Sir John
Perrot took over as President of Munster in 1570 he put an extreme policy into operation, clearing indifferently from the roads
bards and friars, traveling gamblers, craftsmen, and wandering
kern, and dealing with them by the swift processes of martial
law which soon left some eight hundred of them hanging on the
gibbets of Munster.[5] Following on the achievements of Humphrey Gilbert, to which we shall return, the two Tudor phobias
against masterless men and against actual or potential rebels (it
is a single subject in the end) were rarely or so devastatingly
released. In Perrot's lighter moments he amused himself reforming Irish hair styles. "Amongst the rest of my doings here," he
wrote to Burghley in 1573, "I have caused all the Irishry (in
manner) within this province to forgo their glibs, and have
waded into a further danger, as in banishing all the great rolls
from the wearing of ladies, gentlemen, townsmen, and others in
all places." "By which means," he added, "I am assured to have
no wife in these parts." [6] The interference with customary ways
of dress was not as light a thing as it sounded, in spite of the experience of Tudor administrators of the sumptuary legislation of
their own country. Not so dangerous to a culture as the destruction of social groups essential to its working, it could be almost
as productive of resentment and hatred. Sidney's action against
the poets in 1566 opened the way to their outlawry, with results
of which Thomas Churchyard writes:

In this season there was a proclamation made by the Lord Deputy
that whosoever could take a rhymer . . . should spoil him and have

his goods, without danger of law. Master [Nicholas] Malbie, Master Anthony Poore, Master Robert Hartpole, Master Thomas Masterson, being all at Kilkenny, heard of certain blind prophesiers called rhymers that had been abroad with gentlemen and others and gotten their best horses, plate, and jewels for telling them fables and lies, which jewels and treasure came to the value of two hundred marks. These rhymers, going home, were followed by these gentlemen and brought back to Kilkenny and there spoiled and whipped and banished the town, which rhymers swore to rhyme these gentlemen to death, but as yet, God be thanked, they have taken no hurt for punishing such disordered people.[7]

Perrot, severe as he was, was not, either in theory or practice, the most uncompromising of Elizabeth's officials in Ireland. In the Composition of Connacht in the 1580's he showed a masterly understanding of military realities in Gaelic society, and he put a note in the margin of one of his plans for severe repression of Irish law and custom in Munster to say "no extirpation meant." [8] Humphrey Gilbert, however, when he was colonel of the English forces in Munster and military governor of the province, refused to treat at all with the Queen's opponents: if they did not submit when commanded to do so "he killed man, woman, and child," says Churchyard, "and spoiled, wasted, and burned by the ground all that he might." [9] He justified himself by saying that "the men of war could not be maintained without their churls and 'Calliackes' [*cailleacha*, old women], or women who milked their 'Creates' [*creacha*, herds] and provided their victuals and other necessaries. So that the killing of them by the sword was the way to kill the men of war by famine." Gilbert, with powers of martial law at his disposal, could be a bloodthirsty sadist, and Churchyard tells of his revolting practices at this time.

His manner was that the heads of all those . . . which were killed in the day should be cut off from their bodies and brought to the

127

place where he encamped at night, and should there be laid on the ground by each side of the way leading into his own tent, so that none should come into his tent for any cause but commonly he must pass through a lane of heads, which he used *ad terrorem*, the dead feeling nothing the more pains thereby. And yet did it bring great terror to the people when they saw the heads of their dead fathers, brothers, children, kinsfolk, and friends lie on the ground before their faces.

"Which course of government may by some be thought too cruel," Churchyard admits, but says, "in excuse whereof it is to be answered that he did but then begin that order with them which they had in effect ever tofore used toward the English." At the same time the author had pity on Anglo-Irish and Irish alike for the way they were oppressed by the rigors of English military necessity. In his verse letter to Sir Henry Sidney he says:

> The poor, that lives by toil and sweat of brows
> (And near good towns, where each man knows his own),
> Cannot be free nor well enjoy their plows,
> They are indeed with cess so overthrown.
> In any place where proudest people dwell,
> Whose rule is mixed with rage and rigor still,
> Was never seen nor felt so foul an hell
> As this, good Lord, where waste doth what it will.
> Such as be born as free as we ourselves,
> And tills the ground and dearly pays therefor
> (And for their babes full truly digs and delves),
> In their most need we plague and scourge full sore,
> Beyond the course of reason, law, and right.
> A cruel case and twice as heavy a sight
> To see the weak with strongest thrust to wall
> And lose their goods, and not the half but all.
> The people say, were coyne and livery gone
> The land would sure with milk and honey flow:

Their trust is now redress is coming on,
And havoc shall to hateful harbor go.[10]

Such deliberate cruelty as Gilbert's, which went far beyond
the demands of even a severe policy, was exceptional. Yet one of
the more usual failings of the English official in Ireland was
complacency. This led officials to be overoptimistic about the
effects of any vigorously enforced local policy. Thus Perrot,
when bringing his drive against the unruly Irish of Munster
toward a conclusion, wrote to the Queen on July 13, 1573: "The
plow (in this province) doth, through your Majesty's goodness,
now laugh the unbridled kern and rogue to scorn." [11] But after
Perrot had left for England and refused to come back to his
Irish charge, the situation in Munster returned very much to
what it had been before the outbreak of 1569. Complacency also
led Englishmen to blame any disturbance and misery there
might be on anything but English actions. Sir Edward Fitton, at
that time in charge of Connacht, wrote on June 3, 1573: "But
God's will be done, who help this poor land, for the misery
whereof we Englishmen are not in the least guilty." [12] That
these two statements could be made by responsible officials
within a few weeks of each other argues a certain lack of critical
realism on their part, which throws, in turn, a little light on official attitudes in the Irish administration.

Fitton, we saw, denied to Irish society the dignity of a body
politic. Sir John Davies said: "If we consider the nature of the
Irish customs, we shall find that the people which doth use them
must of necessity be rebels to all good government, destroy the
commonwealth wherein they live, and bring barbarism and desolation upon the richest and most fruitful land of the world." [13]
It was attitudes such as these which led Sir Henry Sidney for
example, usually a fair if stern antagonist of Irish "disorder," to
twist the knot of circumstance round Irish necks and use non-
legal methods of repression to make a clean sweep, like Perrot,

129

of local opposition. To the Privy Council he said after a tour of Connacht in April, 1576:

I write not to your Honors the names of each particular varlet that hath died since I arrived, as well by the ordinary course of the law, the martial law, as flat fighting with them when they would take food without the goodwill of the giver, for I think it no stuff worthy the lodging of my letters with to your Lordships. But I do assure you, the number of them is great, and some of the best, and the rest tremble for [the] most part. They fight for their dinner and many of them lose their heads before they be served with their supper. Down they go in every corner, and down they shall go, God willing, if her Majesty will countenance me and your Lordships will comfort me and such as I shall set a-work.[14]

In his state of administrator's euphoria, Sidney is concerned more with the use of force to sweep away all obstacles than with justice or with strict procedure according to law. His sights are set on an allover plan of pacification, as he would have thought it—asserting on another occasion that "if forcible subjection, which I like better than any other proceeding, be best allowed, I will rather hold that course." [15] He had in his mind's eye a picture of what could be done with Sir William Drury and the Earl of Essex, as Presidents in Munster and Connacht respectively, "as two good wheels holding up the South and West end of this realm's axletree." As for himself, "I will so deal, I hope, with the East and North as the wain of Ireland shall bring harvest merely home within very few years, though not to England's gain, yet without England's charge." These brave, encouraging words he was perhaps to regret when he left Ireland for the last time in 1578, ill and disheartened but not, it would seem, fully conscious that repression alone was unlikely to bring permanent settlement to a society he had failed, despite much effort, effectively to understand.

If there was the temptation to use any and every method to deal with the presumed excesses and anomalies of Irish society,

so too there was a tendency to excuse such attitudes by imput-
ing to Irishmen qualities which rendered justifiable action that
would otherwise have seemed unprincipled. Treachery was one
such imputation. Lord Grey of Wilton, when Lord Deputy in
1581, wrote that he did not care to receive submissions from
Irish lords who had been in arms against the government. He
described the receiving of submissions and the granting of par-
dons as "a course not the surest for the state, because the Irish
are so addicted to treachery and breach of fidelity as, longer
than they find the yoke [is] in their neck, they respect not either
pledge, affinity, or duty." [16] This is very much the attitude taken
earlier by Gilbert. Grey himself was thought by some Englishmen to have proved treacherous at Smerwick to the papal force
he conquered there, and belief in his cruelty was general
enough among English observers to lead Spenser to make an
impassioned defense of him in his *View* in 1596.[17] This is not to
deny that Irish lords could be untrustworthy, but, in the long
battle of wits which accompanied the intermittent wars, double-
dealing was an almost inevitable weapon for them to use when
faced with unacceptable proposals involving the surrender of
traditional institutions and usages. Belief on either side in the
untrustworthiness of the other was one of the reasons for the
length of the wars with Tyrone at the end of the reign.

Irish intransigence and uprisings meant hardship and suffering, alike for loyal Old English and Irish who stood at the side
of the English administrators and soldiers. The soldiers found
Irish warfare physically arduous and disease-ridden: long inde-
cisive campaigns wore down any objections they had to the general massacre of civilians. In a war of attrition, the Irish population, if hard finally to pin down and defeat, gradually suffered
immensely. It was easy to remark, as many Englishmen did,
that it was only necessary for Irishmen to fly with their families
to the woods and mountains to avoid English vengeance, but
Irish life was not so loosely rooted or nomadic that enforced

flight could not wreck its economy and inflict great hardships.
While the O Neills of Clandeboye were, in 1573, able to escape
the attentions of the Earl of Essex' army, a winter in the woods
left them in bad shape. Edward Barkley, one of Essex' would-be
planters, on outpost duty at Belfast in May, 1574, wrote:

They have no kind of grain, nor hath sown so much as two plows
will till. In Clandeboye their sheep are devoured with wolves and
stealths with keeping them so long in the woods, so as they have no
wool to make them mantles, coats, nor hose. Their exchange of
dwellings have been such as they are altogether without flax or means
to make linen cloth. Nor traffic they have in no place but a little
with the Scots, who are daily ready to fly from them. How these
people are able to continue any time, I cannot imagine.[18]

Each new phase of disturbance seemed to give rise to harsher
views and to more sanguinary policies. The Desmond rising of
1579–1583 marked a further sharpening of English methods of
winning victory by the wearing down of the civilian population
and so, in the end, depriving the mobile Irish soldiery of food
and recruits. John Hooker reported that after the wiping out of
the papal force in 1580 the people of the district surrounding
Smerwick were reduced to eating human flesh, so severe was
the clearance of farmers and livestock from the area.[19] Spenser's
description of the end result for the Irish inhabitants of four
years of Munster warfare and clearances is, perhaps, not too
well-known to be cited:

They were brought to such wretchedness as that any stony heart
would have rued the same. Out of every corner of the woods and
glens they came creeping forth upon their hands, for their legs would
not bear them. They looked anatomies of death; they spake like
ghosts crying out of their graves. They did eat of the dead car-
rions, . . . and if they found a plot of watercresses or shamrocks
there they flocked as to a feast for the time, yet not able long to
continue therewithal, [so] that in short space there were none almost

left and a most populous and plentiful country suddenly left \
man and beast.[20]

Though not written until 1596, this has lost nothing of it\
idness or horror. At the time, in 1583, Sir James Croft laid the
blame fairly on the military methods adopted, which he considered quite unjustifiable. He denounced, without qualification,
"these unexpert captains and soldiers that hath slain and destroyed as well the unarmed as armed, even to the plowman
that never bare weapon, extending cruelty upon both sexes and
upon all ages, from the babe in the cradle to the decrepit age, in
sort not to be named and by Christian people not to be looked
upon." [21]

Yet a kind of peace was attained in the decade after 1585 as
Munster settled into a plantation and Connacht achieved an apparent equilibrium under a rationalized form of military taxation adapted from the Irish system, and while, too, Hugh O Neill,
before and after he attained the title of Earl of Tyrone in
1587, maintained a pacific policy behind which his effective
strength grew. A new wave of optimism flowed across the minds
of some Englishmen. Richard Beacon, formerly the Queen's attorney in Munster, addressed Queen Elizabeth in 1594 in confident tones. Had not Ireland become populous and well-
governed, with beautiful cities and towns?

What more? Have you not reformed all exactions grievous unto that
people? Have you not reformed that horrible and most detestable
custom of coyne and livery, that fretter of the people's lives and
substance, that nurse and teat which sometimes gave suck and nutri-
ment unto all disobedience, rebellions, enormities, vices, and iniqui-
ties of that realm, overfoul and filthy here to be expressed? Have
you not in place of sorrow, famine, howling, and cursing brought
joy, jollity, plenty, and everywhere blessings of so gracious a Queen?
Have you not reformed that dangerous custom of captainship [Irish
lordship], which by factions did dismember the state of Ireland?
. . . You have changed the life of man, which before your time was

rude, cruel, and wild in Ireland, and brought it for the most part to
be obedient, gentle, and civil, in such sort as we may truly say with
the subject of Ireland, "This is the favor which your Majesty hath
found in the sight of God, to augment, strengthen, and honor your
imperial crown of England by the thorough reformation of this your
realm of Ireland." [22]

So much rhetoric would not perhaps be worth citing—though it
is revealing—if it was not so much at variance with the rest of
the tract and with the circumstances of the time. Beacon is elsewhere concerned to point out the many and various precautions
by law and force which must still be taken by both officials and
soldiers against Irish raids and assaults. In his discourse he both
stresses the need for the firm and fair administration of English
law and commends Sir Richard Bingham, stern President of
Connacht, for failing to follow strictly legal practices. Bingham,
"another Caesar," had captured some recalcitrant Irishmen but,
Beacon says, "seeing himself fallen into these extremities, that
either he must spare the lives of open and manifest rebels, to the
damage of the commonweal, or execute them without lawful in-
dictment and other ceremonies, like a wise governor . . . made
choice of the least." [23] The men were executed and, indeed, the
regime of force rather than law was thereby demonstrated. The
other major discrepancy between Beacon's theory and Irish circumstance was that, even as the tract was being written, new
disturbances had begun in the north of Ireland and were already leading toward the bloody and long-sustained conflict
that lasted from 1594 to 1603.

The Nine Years' War, 1594–1603, was not one of continuous
fighting. Until 1598 it was localized in Ulster and was inter-
rupted by frequent truces. But even in 1597 we find it said that
"the country is impoverished even to the bones." [24] From 1598
onward it became general over much of the island. The war of
attrition waged by the great English forces sent over had al-

ready done great havoc by the time the Spaniards arrived, in too small force, to aid the Irish at Kinsale in 1601. After their defeat and that of the Ulster lords with them, the struggle gradually wore down to an end. O Donnell left Ireland for Spain after Kinsale and died there in 1602. Tyrone's tenacity kept him in the field until March, 1603, when he at last agreed to come to terms with the Queen. Though she was now dead, Lord Mountjoy, as we saw, clinched the arrangement before letting O Neill know the truth.

These are vastly documented years, so that to pick out impressions from the mass of papers is, almost certainly, to work more at random even than before. What is clear is that statesmen in England, officials in Ireland, and English soldiers in the field found Ireland and the Irish grow steadily more obnoxious to them as the war went on. Lord Hunsdon, who had possibly been with Essex in County Antrim in 1573, wrote of the island in 1597 as "the accursed kingdom of Ireland," [25] while Sir Robert Cecil, who as Secretary of State had more to do with it than any other English statesman, got into the habit of calling it "the land of Ire." [26] "There have been by many of us Englishmen a hard opinion held of all Irishmen since this action," said an anonymous writer in 1599, "and some will say, 'If he be an Irishman, he will have an Irish trick,'" while "the poor English [the rank and file of the soldiery, he means] are half dead before they come there, for the very name of Ireland do break their hearts, it is now grown to such a misery." [27] The English soldier, indeed, was capable of expressing his own sharp reaction against, at least, some groups in Irish society. Gervase Markham had just returned from Irish service in 1600 when he wove a long episode about the Irish kern into his rambling poem, "The New Metamorphosis." [28] He gives the kern a scandalous ancestry. Originally fit occupants of an Irish Sodom, they were, when their town of Kerne for its licentiousness was submerged be-

135

neath the waters of Lough Erne, transformed into wolves, whose most recent descendants still had the capacity to put on human shape and be almost men, or rather kern, again:

> The kerns sprung thus from this prodigious brood
> Are still as lewd as when their city stood.
> Fraught with all vice, replete with villainy,
> They still rebel and that most treacherously.
> Like brutish Indians these wild Irish live;
> Their quiet neighbors they delight to grieve.
> Cruel and bloody, barbarous and rude,
> Dire vengeance at their heels hath them pursued.
> They are the savagest of all the nation;
> Amongst them out I made my peregrination,
> Where many wicked customs I did see
> Such as all honest hearts I hope will flee.

Current English verses, as we might expect, became ever more bitter as the war went on. An anonymous verse writer in 1600, developing the Tudor "order" theme, "Obedience joins; Disorder separates," spoke of the Irish:

> Yet these blind reprobates, *Megora's* brats,
> These saffron shirts; these parti-pleated jacks:
> These wood-born savages; these dunghill gnats,
> Had rather bear war armor on their backs
> (So they may practice rapes, and true men's wracks)
> Than freely take fair Mercy by the hand,
> To glad themselves and dignify their land.[29]

After the English had defeated the belated Spanish attempt to assist the insurgent Irish at Kinsale in 1601, the tone becomes at once more fierce and more confident. Another pamphleteer wrote at this time:

> The Irish rebels now do keep their caves
> Amid the woods like wolves or ravening beasts;
> Where all like outlaws or uncivil slaves

On grass and shamrocks now they make their feasts.
O England, never better news can be
Than this to hear, how God doth fight for thee.[30]

The official view, put out by the Queen and her ministers, offers something of a contrast, which may be illustrated from the proclamation of March 31, 1599,[31] announcing the dispatch of Essex to Ireland, to end, as it was believed, the war in England's favor. The Queen stresses "how earnestly we have affected the peace and the tranquillity of the people of our dominions," but how, despite this, divers subjects of the kingdom of Ireland "have committed many bloody and violent outrages." Even though "ways have been attempted to reclaim them by clemency," there have so far been no results, as there would have been had there been on the rebels' part "any sense of religion, duty, or common humanity." Some men have, it is true, been forced into disloyalty by "the wicked and barbarous rebels," who have alleged, falsely, "that we intended an utter extirpation and rooting out of that nation and Conquest of the country." The document continues, "The very name of Conquest in this case seemeth absurd to us," since the object of military action was only "to reduce a number of unnatural and barbarous rebels and to root out the capital heads of the most notorious traitors." Why this should "need any such title of Conquest" is not evident, when "the best part of our nobility, the people of all our good towns, and divers of our subjects" are assured in their loyalty. Subjects in rebellion are reminded of "the extreme misery whereunto they shall throw themselves." The army and its commander, the Earl of Essex, are therefore to minister "both of our justice and mercy." The assumption all through the proclamation was that Ireland was a single society, occupied by a homogeneous people. It is true that there were Irish lords and soldiers on the English side throughout and that Tyrone's party in the end contained a number of Old English magnates, but what was at stake, as all knew, was in a real sense the survival of an autonomous Gaelic society, and conquest, whatever the Queen might say, was hoped for and intended.

But Essex failed, Mountjoy came in. Fynes Moryson, his chronicler, saw "the rebellion was at the greatest strength," when he was appointed in 1600: "The mere Irish, puffed up with good success and blooded with happy encounters, did boldly keep the field and proudly disdain the English forces. Great part of the English-Irish were in open action of rebellion and most part of the rest temporized with the state." [32] Mountjoy had the men, the money, the arms, the strategic conceptions necessary to box Tyrone into his own lands, and, above all, he had confidence in himself. When he heard the Spaniards had landed at Kinsale his reaction, in a letter to Cecil, was to say, "I cannot dissemble how confident I am to beat these Spanish Dons as well as ever I did our Irish 'Macks and Oes' and to make a perfect conclusion of the war of Ireland." [33] Nor did he ever let himself, his troops, or the Irish have any respite until victory was certain. On February 25, 1603, he admitted his preference when the war was won was that "I should . . . either have made this country a rased table, wherein she [the Queen] might have written her own laws, or have tied the ill-disposed and rebellious hands till I had surely planted such a government as would have overgrown and killed any weeds that should have risen under it" [34]—that is, he aimed at a complete conquest and a new start, with Irish Ireland swept away. In the event, since his money and his men did not extend quite far enough, he did not recommend too great severity in the settlement for the time being.[35] He took this course rather because he had too little confidence that English colonies scattered over the whole of Ireland could rapidly take effect than because he favored any fundamental accommodation with the Irish. Yet now, with the new strength which the English had, the Irish were to be kept to the letter of their engagements and turned out of their lands if they were in any way negligent or recalcitrant. Colonies might be inserted where they had the best prospects, so that "a future absolute reducement of this country" could be kept in mind.

Throughout the war, sympathy with the Irish did not die entirely amongst the English. The fact that "the good subjects," the Irish and Old English not in arms against England, were still an influence in the land was apparent to a number of Englishmen. Sir William Warren told Cecil on December 5, 1599, that the Irish "are not such devils as they are thought to be." [36] Nor was there silence about the oppression of the English soldiery, who, in July, 1598, we hear "make havoc and spoil of the poor inhabitants and subjects of the land, which is now so wretched and miserable as the poor souls that are left have nothing else to feed upon but roots, grasses, and boiled nettles." [37] Mountjoy was, compared with Perrot and Gilbert and even Sidney, a humane man who did not engage in senseless and inhuman massacre of noncombatants: "I am loath to make war with women," he said on one occasion. But he also admitted that when he came to Ireland in 1601 he was at a loss how to bring Irish resistance to an end, and so "I presumed that man's wit could hardly find out any other course to overcome them but by famine." [38] Consequently, as his forces bored into Ulster they gradually devastated the land and killed the cattle they found. The result can be judged from the report of a contemporary chronicler, William Farmer, of the plight of the people of Ulster in 1601:

In this year happened a great famine and scarcity of victuals in the North, as well among the English as the Irish. . . . Sir Arthur Chichester . . . as he traveled through a wood . . . felt a great savor, as it were roasting or broiling of flesh; the governor sent out soldiers to search the wood, and they found a cabin where a woman was dead, and five children by her made fire to her thighs and arms and sides, roasting her flesh and eating it. The governor went to the place to see it, and demanded of them why they did so; they answered they could not get any other meat. It was demanded where their cows were, and they said the Englishmen had taken them away. Also it was demanded when the woodkern were there, and they answered not in three days before. It was asked of them whether they would have meat or money to relieve them; they answered both meat and money; so the governor commanded to collect a proportion of victuals from among the soldiers' knapsacks, and left it with them, and so departed.[39]

For the year 1603, when peace came at last—the peace of death and exhaustion to many—Fynes Moryson is able to add other horrifying pictures. After a local composition with the Irish had been made, it was, he says, a common practice for the starving Irishmen "to thrust long needles into the horses of our English troops" so that when the beasts were dead they were "ready to tear out one another's throat for a share of them." He goes on to remark that "no spectacle was more frequent in the ditches of towns, and especially in wasted countries, than to see multitudes of these poor people dead, with their mouths all colored green by eating nettles, docks, and all things they could rend up above ground." He relates another grim tale of the country near Newry, County Down:

Some old women of those parts used to make a fire in the fields, and divers little children, driving out the cattle in the cold mornings and coming thither to warm them[selves], were by them surprised, killed, and eaten. Which at last was discovered by a great girl breaking from them by strength of her body, and Captain Trevor sending out soldiers to know the truth, they found the children's skulls and bones and apprehended the old women, who were executed for the fact.[40]

Only O Neill's submission saved the remainder of the people of Ulster, Moryson thought, from death by famine: by it they were released, he said, "to seek relief among the subjects of Ireland and to be transported into England and France, where great numbers of them lived for some years after the peace was made."

140

In 1603 the end of the old Irish social system had indeed come. The brehons would be pushed to one side. The lands would be divided in private ownership under primogeniture. English officials would supervise the Irish areas, English garrisons guard them. The gradual elimination of the Catholic religion would be next. When O Neill and the younger O Donnell found they could not tolerate this state of affairs, they fled from Ireland in 1607, thus opening up the greater part of Ulster to the lawyers, who transferred title to the lands to King James, whose loyal subjects from England and Scotland moved in as colonists in the next few years. A new spreading of English landowners and townsmen was laid on Munster too, and other lands changed hands by confiscation in the next decade or so. In 1625 Ireland was a country where old colonists, New English, and Irish each owned about a third of the property. The Protestant state church was installed over the whole island: the laws were English.

Maire MacEntee has salvaged two quatrains from Irish poets of the time and turned them into neat, ironic, savage comments of the defeated:

> May we never taste of death nor quit this vale of tears
> Until we see the Englishry go begging down the years,
> Packs on their backs to earn a penny pay,
> In little leaking boots, as we went in our day.
>
> Time has o'erthrown, the wind has blown away
> Alastair, Caesar, such great names as they—
> See Troy and Tara where in grass they lie—
> Even the very English might yet die! [41]

By 1614 Lord Carew was willing to admit that "the mere Irish (by their travel abroad) are civilized, grown to be disciplined soldiers, scholars, politicians, and further instructed on points of religion than accustomed." [42] But this was not necessarily, from the English point of view, a cause for congratulation, since it meant, amongst other things, that "the old English race," which had "despised the mere Irish, accounting them to be a barbarous people," were now more willing to lay aside "the ancient dislike and contempt" which had kept them apart. Conquest was, indeed, helping to link Irish and Old English in a unity born out of common suffering.

CHAPTER XI

The Irishman Translated

MOVEMENT across the Irish Sea was not in one direction only. Probably more Englishmen came to and went from Ireland in Elizabethan times than Irishmen came to England. But we do not know. Irishmen played some part in the English scene from before the beginning of the Tudor period: they were playing a substantial part in the later sixteenth century. Yet the course of their migration is still almost wholly uncharted. Nor do we even know at all precisely how the image of the Irishman—and the Irishwoman—seen in London, for example, changed in detail over the sixteenth century.

Under Henry VII, Irishmen appear from time to time bringing messages or gifts—hawks, dogs, hobbies (riding horses)—to the King, but the major comings and goings recorded between Ireland and London were those of the great lords from the Anglicized parts of Ireland and their children and dependents. But these Old English magnates, Earls of Kildare or Ormond, had Irishmen among their attendants as personal servants, footmen, horseboys, and others in mainly menial positions. There was much contact by sea between ports like Bristol, Milford, and Chester with Irish shipping, but this too was largely owned by Old English merchants of the eastern and southern port towns and sometimes manned by Old English crews. There was, inevitably, some Irish settlement in English ports. Bristol had an Irish quarter: merchants from Ireland sent their sons to be apprentices to many Bristol crafts [1]—but they, too, were mainly Old English by birth. The impression from the very imperfect evidence available is that, whatever may have been the case in the late twelfth and thirteenth centuries, in the late fifteenth and early sixteenth centuries contact between Gaelic Ireland and England was small and Irish lords were much more likely, if they left their home territory, to visit continental Europe rather than England, while most of their subjects were also unlikely to have contacts with England which would make them come and go across the Irish Sea. The exception to these generalizations, if they are that and not mere guesses, is that the singers, the jugglers, and the beggars who roved the Irish roads were not unlikely to try their luck in England from time to time if opportunity offered and to get into the way of returning occasionally for fresh adventures, or even settling in the end into some niche in an English town or village. The visit of Manus O Donnell to the court of the young Henry VIII on his way homeward from Rome in 1511 was an event which the chroniclers thought worth stressing because it was so unusual.[2] Occasionally there was a scare that Irishmen were crowding into lands in the West. An excitable Welshman wrote in 1528 that 20,000 Irishmen had entered Pembrokeshire in the past twelve months, had virtually taken over the town of Tenby, had entered the service of local men, and had practically overrun the county.[3] He seems to have made mountains out of molehills, for the respectable borough of Tenby does not seem to have been in any degree permanently Hibernicized nor, indeed, does anyone but the writer seem to have seen these great numbers of invading "Irish rascals." But the incident, even if the reporter was somewhat paranoiac, does underline the fact that intercourse between the two islands was, at their extremities, close and constant. The sea was the open road at this time, and journeys across St. George's Channel to fairs or markets on either side was a practicable proposition. It is also true, however, that the men of Wexford or Waterford who might come and go most freely in West Wales were Old English rather than Irish. It is likely that the traffic across the Irish Sea was partly seasonal, Irishmen coming over to travel the roads or work in summer and returning later in the year. Haymaking and harvesting may already, though this is not firmly established, have begun to attract them. The report that an official in Dublin in 1536 took "a fleece of all poor men that come from Ireland" [4] to England might suggest a seasonal traffic.

A major change took place after 1534 with the establishment of an English executive in Dublin and with English diplomacy and armies winning access to a much larger part of the country. The policy of surrender and re-grant and the assumption of the kingship by Henry VIII provided the occasion for much more movement to London by Irish lords and their retinues than there had been for a long time. Between 1541 and 1543 there was a procession of lords who came to make their submission to the King, promising to serve him and to give up their Irish dress and, as far as possible, to use the English language, while receiving in turn English titles. The greatest impression was made by Con O Neill, whose creation as Earl of Tyrone by the King on September 24, 1542, was the occasion for a pamphlet, the first separate printed item to be devoted to Ireland by an English press.[5] Magnates were soon followed by Irish soldiers, six hundred kern being brought through England to take part in the fighting for Boulogne in 1544, where they created a lasting impression by their belligerence. Richard Eden, introducing his *Treatise of the New India* in 1553, notes how "a man unarmed slew a man armed, as did sometime the wild Irishmen at Boulogne." [6] Others were detailed for garrison duty on the Scottish borders. Sons of Irish magnates were sent to Court to be brought up in the English manner, as was Barnaby Fitzpatrick, whose father had been created Lord Upper Ossory. Or it might be that when an Irish lord failed to maintain good relations with the Dublin government, he would arrive as a prisoner destined for the Tower, as Brian O Conor Faly did in 1548. Masques and plays on Irish themes are known to have been presented at Court between 1551 and 1557, showing a continued lively interest in Irishmen.[7]

The beginnings of a deep religious rift came in Edward VI's reign with the adoption of Protestantism in England, and at the very least it made relations with the Irish lords much less easy. It also tended to make Irishmen coming to or living in England fall under some suspicion as Catholics: they were unlikely, for example, to obey the act of 1559 requiring them, as the Queen's subjects, to attend the established church, and it was quite probable that they would attend Mass if they found an opportunity to do so. Indeed, in 1572, "certain Irishmen, students of the law," were imprisoned on the orders of the Bishop of London for attending Mass at the house of the Portuguese ambassador.[8] But the Privy Council intervened to have them released. Most, but not all, of these students would be from Old English rather than Irish families, and it was clear that if they were dragooned into becoming even nominal Protestants their parents would no longer send them to continue their education in England. They would go instead, and many did so, to Catholic colleges on the Continent, where, as the religious struggle became even more embittered, they were, for the most part, turned into enemies of the Queen and, perhaps, into missioners for the maintenance of Irish Catholic zeal.

The Earl of Ormond, when he wished to disparage Irishmen who were living in London but yet did not enjoy the full privileges of citizenship, said in 1576 that there were "multitudes of poor men of Ireland who are free men of divers mean crafts" in the city.[9] There were also apprentices from Ireland in the more respectable trades—two of them, for example, were accepted by the Stationers' Company in 1566.[10] These indications point to

the growth of a sizable Irish population of a permanent character in London. There was also a more shifting and less welcome
one in the Irish wandering beggars who were frequently seen in
Elizabethan London. They were so much a symbol of distress
that the French ambassador, Castelnau de la Mauvissière,
searching for an object to express the plight of Condé in 1585,
compared him with "those exiled Irish who solicit alms in England with their children by their sides." [11]

The Irishman did not find it easy to obtain tolerance as a beggar in the English countryside. He had no status which would
enable him to claim the privileges of a begging license such as
was accorded, for example, to mutilated former soldiers and
sailors. Consequently he was liable to be seized, imprisoned, and
perhaps subjected to severe physical punishment as well as a jail
sentence if he was captured by the authorities, who were always
on the lookout for able-bodied unemployed men to terrorize and
punish. Consequently, Irishmen on English roads found means
to obtain forged licenses with which they might deceive at least
the village constables as they moved about. Thomas Harman,
who did a remarkable survey of beggars in the early years of
Elizabeth's reign, reported: "There be many Irishmen that go
about with counterfeit licenses, and if they perceive you will
straitly [i.e., strictly] examine them, they will immediately say
they can speak no English." [12] He also exposed the "fresh-water
mariners" whose "ships were drowned in the plains of Salisbury"
and who, running around the country equipped with forged licenses, "counterfeit great losses on the sea." "These be some
western men and most be Irishmen," he commented.[13] A local
calamity in Ireland, the outbreak of violence in a particular
area, for example, might send a scattering of Irish men and
women to beg on the roads of England. "There is above an hundred of Irish men and women," Harman reported, "that wander
about to beg for their living that hath come over within these
two years [he is writing about 1566]. They say they have been

burned and spoiled by the Earl of Desmond and report well of the Earl of Ormond." [14] Harman equipped his book with long lists of beggars, specifying their particular roguish tricks. Only four Irishmen, however, figure there by name.[15] This might suggest that their pretended ignorance of the English language served them in good stead in that it was not so easy, if they maintained it, to pin an identity on them. Another possible explanation is that they were for the most part simple beggars only and did not go in for the more specialized deceptions which Harman was most concerned to expose.

When the Lord Mayor of London wrote to the Privy Council in 1583 [16] about the poverty-stricken Irish who frequented the city, he looked at them, as Harman had done, more as a social nuisance than as a deserving class. He had rounded up a number of them and had them in prison in Bridewell. He asked for permission to send them back to Ireland, and he also requested that no more Irishmen (at least of their sort) should be allowed to come to England. This was easier to say than to do, and the English government did not attempt to enforce any general embargo against Irish immigrants. Nor was it always, in every circumstance, unwilling to countenance begging by the Irish in England. This, when it was licensed as the soliciting of alms, could be made respectable. In 1591, "three poor Irishwomen that had been long suitors [applying for some legal redress from the Council], having dispatched their business here," were licensed, while on their way "into their native country . . . to gather by the way as they pass the charitable devotions of well-disposed people," [17] that is, to beg their way home. The next year, 1592, another suitor, William Englishe, was given a rather different type of concession after he had been kept waiting for a long time to get a decision on his case. To repopulate his estates, which had been largely deserted by his tenants during his absence in England, he was allowed to take with him seventeen adults and some children from amongst "the great numbers of vagrant and masterless persons of Irish birth . . . [who] a long time . . . go begging in and about the city of London," and who had been already imprisoned for that offense.[18] It seems not at all unlikely that, as wars, raids, and counter-raids developed in Ireland throughout the latter part of Elizabeth's reign, more impoverished Irish people were encouraged to go begging in England to obtain any livelihood at all. A character of Dekker's reflects what was clearly a common attitude when he says that the Irish in England swarm "like crickets to the crevice of a brewhouse." [19] If there was indeed such an increase, the Tudor phobia against the masterless man was no doubt especially aroused by the mobile Irish poor.

Irishmen emerge in English records from time to time on criminal charges more serious than begging. An extract from the Liverpool records for 1565 shows us an Irish purse-stealer caught and punished.

This year [on] Sunday at night, after supper, the ninth of this December, was one Patrick Fyn, an Irish born in the Queen's County, lackey late in the Earl [of] Ormond's livery, out of service, taken for cutting a purse of one of the fine gentlemen that went to Ireland with my Lord Deputy Sidney's company, in which was jewels and gold to the value of five pounds, all had again, for he was taken with the purse. . . . And he was prisoned that night and, after his examination, nailed to a post by the ear and so whipped out of the town naked from the middle upwards.[20]

Patrick Fyn's fate was no better or no worse than if he had been an Englishman, but it illustrates the harsh summary justice of the time. More exceptional was the case which disturbed the Chester authorities in 1602–1603.[21] An Irish boy, attending a French gentlemen on his journey through England, stole his purse at Chester. The young man was helped on his way out of the city but was arrested as he was about to sail for Ireland. At the same time, a Chester curate, Lawrence Bradshaw, whose name does not suggest that he had any Irish connections, was imprisoned for assisting the boy to escape. The culprit induced his former master to take pity on him and not to press charges, so that he was released and eventually taken back into service. This left Bradshaw in grave difficulties; he could no longer be charged as an accessory to a crime where the principal had not been tried, and so was released, but, as the mayor said, "He is undone, for he hath been degraded from the ministry by the bishop." If this was an example of tenderheartedness by an Englishman toward an Irishman in trouble (though it is not certain that Bradshaw did not put a price on his help), it cost him dear.

Irish quarrelsomeness sometimes produced violence in England even at a high level of society. Arnold Cosby, "an Irishman," fell out with his friend John, Lord Bourke, Baron of Castle Connell, head of a recently ennobled Old English family. Being unable to fight out his quarrel in the streets of London, Cosby challenged Bourke to a duel on Wandsworth Common. The men met without seconds on January 14, 1592, when Cosby, unable to restrain himself, attacked his adversary before he was ready, ran him through, it was alleged, twenty-three times after the initial thrust, and left him for dead. Bourke survived long enough to accuse his assailant to the Earl of Essex and other influential men. Consequently Cosby was tried and hanged, the events being commemorated by one of Bourke's servants in a news pamphlet.[22]

Yet from time to time when an arduous task was undertaken, the reputation of Irishmen for hard work and for certain craftsmen's skills led to their employment in England in some numbers. In 1560 two hundred "good and fit masons and hewers of rough stone" were ordered to be assembled in Ireland to be employed on Queen Elizabeth's fortifications at Berwick-on-Tweed.[23] A number of men were duly sent and in April and May, 1563, they were on their way home, their task completed. "The Irish masons, well paid," we are told, "came to Liverpool for shipping into Ireland, their native country. And here in Liverpool they bestowed part of their money and appareled themselves honestly, many of them," [24] that is, they bought and put on English clothes, going home Anglicized at least in externals.

Indeed, there is a good deal of evidence that Irishmen were regarded by many Englishmen as hard and faithful workers when in England, and that a substantial number were in the employment of members of the gentry and nobility. Officials and soldiers, back from Ireland, frequently brought with them Irish personal attendants, footmen and grooms in particular, and they were prized as such, Dr. J. O. Bartley suggests, "partly for their efficiency, partly for their exotic quality, and partly as concrete evidence of English domination." [25] He shows that in real life, as in the Elizabethan theater, the Irish footman retained in England his long hair (the glib already noticed), his tight trousers, and his stafflike "dart" or horse rod. The Irishmen's skill in tending the horses, dogs, and hawks brought from Ireland endeared them to many of their masters. Animals from Ireland also were treated almost as if they were Irishmen. Gabriel Harvey made a note of "Master William Smyth's watchword to his great white Irish hobby—'Mack Dei, Mack Diaboli' [*MacDé, mac diabhail*]." [26] Irish gardeners, too, worked on English estates. Even the anonymous author of a project of 1599 for opening up Ireland to English settlement by distributing the bulk of the Irish population over England, under English masters, conceded that

in England we find the Irish servant very faithful and loving, and generally the people kind, the rather when here their malice [that is, their resistance to English activities in Ireland] cannot profit them any way. Withal they be here industrious, and commonly our best gardeners, fruiterers, and keepers of our horses, refusing no labor besides.[27]

The Elizabethans and the Irish

The reference to the Irish as "fruiterers" is borne out by frequent literary references to the Irish costermonger,[28] though no convincing explanation has yet been found of why the Irish should have so nearly monopolized this occupation. It was probably one of the "mean trades" exercised by the Irish in London, as already mentioned. It may be that it, and another occupation which largely seems to have fallen, in the capital at least, into Irish hands—that of chimney sweeping—did so because they lacked effective guild organization and were therefore, and perhaps also by their peripatetic character, attractive to Irishmen. But where personal service and fruit selling were respectable, if usually lowly, occupations in Elizabethan England, chimney sweeping was regarded as somewhat degrading and may be held to illustrate the assumption by the despised immigrant of a socially undesirable task which was not sought after by the home population. When Anthony Chute is recording in 1595 the anti-tobacco sentiments of some Englishmen, he cites one of them as saying: "Happily someone as wise as a woodcock will raise his flight on his beck and cry, 'Fie, fie, how it stinks! Smell you it not?' or tell me he will hire an Irishman to chimney sweep my stomach." [29]

Irishmen, too, might act the fool, but they were thought to keep their wits about them. Moryson tells us that Lord Mountjoy to his dying day "kept an Irishman in fool's apparel and commonly called his lordship's fool. . . . But we found him," he continues, "to have craft of humoring every way to attain his own ends and to have nothing of a natural fool." [30]

Just as the visit of Con O Neill had made a sharp impression on the English consciousness in 1542, so the mission of Shane O Neill—his successor and in English eyes an illegitimate one—to Queen Elizabeth in 1562 impinged sharply on Elizabethan London. William Camden, who was a schoolboy eleven years old at the time of the visit, put it on record in his *History* [31] as follows:

The Irishman Translated

Now was Shane O Neal come out of Ireland to perform what he had promised a year before, with a guard of ax-bearing galloglasses, bareheaded, with curled hair hanging down, yellow surplices [the Irish shirts] dyed with saffron or man's stale [urine], long sleeves, short coats, and hairy mantles. Whom the English people gazed at with no less admiration [he adds with a touch of later sophistication] than nowadays they do them of China and America.*

Shane's submission to the Queen, in the presence of the ambassadors of Sweden and the Duke of Savoy, as well as many English nobles, was humble enough in form, but the courtiers, Edmund Campion tells us in 1571, were sarcastic about his pride and what seemed to them his pretensions, calling him "Oneale the great, cousin to St. Patrick, friend to the Queen of England, enemy to all the world besides." [32] We have glimpses of him riding to dine with a goldsmith in the City, learning to ride in the English fashion, tilting, hawking, and shooting with Lord Robert Dudley,[33] soon to be Earl of Leicester, to whom he afterward sent presents of hawks, horses, and greyhounds, as he was no mean diplomat.[34] William Cecil, the Queen's Secretary of State, thought it a bad advertisement for the government's policy of putting down the use of Irish dress and customs like wearing the glib that they should be flaunted in London,[35] but there was nothing, for the moment, he could do about it. None of the ballads doubtless published about Shane appear to have survived, but he was revived from time to time as a type figure of the "wild Irish" magnate. His visit perhaps suggested the figure in Thomas Hughes's play, The Misfortunes of Arthur (1587), described as "a man bareheaded, with black, long, shagged hair down to his shoulders, appareled with an Irish

* Cavendish brought two Japanese to court in 1588, but I do not know of any Chinese being there in Elizabeth's reign. Manteo and Wanchese, brought from Roanoke Island in 1584, were observed at Court in the winter of 1584–1585 by a German visitor. Cf. D. B. Quinn, The Roanoke Voyages, I, 116.

jacket and shirt, having an Irish dagger by his side and a dart in his hand"; [36] even perhaps a ballad, entered in 1588 (also lost), "The valiant deeds of MacCab an Irishman." [37] *The Irish Knight,* a play seen by Queen Elizabeth in 1577, may also have owed something to Shane.[38]

There were other Irish lords in London too, later in the reign, but they never created such a stir or made so deep an impression. In any event, they were usually young boys coming over to be brought up in English ways—Hugh O Neill, later the most formidable of all the Irish opponents of Elizabethan supremacy, lived from 1559 to 1566 with the Sidneys in England [39]—or they were prisoners in the Tower for what the English considered their unruly conduct in Ireland, although some whose presence was considered a precaution rather than a punishment were left free on condition that they lived in London and did not attempt to return to their Irish estates. Barnaby Rich in 1591 even thought it might be worthwhile bringing a substantial number of the Irish nobility to England, there to remain, although they might be allowed to have their Irish revenues sent to them.[40] Enforced absenteeism of this sort appears to have been exceptional rather than usual, while it is not clear that any of the Irish gentlemen detained for a time in England settled down permanently there.

Young Irishmen from princely families retained in England at one of the universities were liable to be torn between their studies and their duties in Ireland: it was difficult for them to know whether they would be permitted to return home even temporarily. Sir Donough O Connor Sligo had been presented with a gold brooch by Queen Elizabeth at his departure to Ireland in the summer of 1569, but his brother Owen was left behind in Oxford University. Sir Donough wrote asking him to come home at once as their lordship was being attacked by their enemies. Owen asked the Queen to give him permission to do so, emphasizing that this was an emergency and that he had no wish to leave Oxford for good.[41] Normally, such permission would be refused, as the young man would be regarded as a hostage for his family's good behavior. Yet Sir Brian O Rourke, for all that his son was still a student at Oxford, found himself in arms against the Crown in 1589. On his defeat he sought refuge in Scotland but was handed over to Queen Elizabeth by James VI. He was duly tried as a traitor and executed at Tyburn in November, 1591.[42]

Irish suits and suitors at the Queen's Court, which figure prominently in English documents of the time, did not necessarily involve Irishmen alone. Many, if not most, were petitions by Englishmen for rewards for Irish service or requests for jobs or perquisites in Ireland. Others were pleas in legal cases, or political ones, perhaps, from Old English gentlemen or merchants for the righting of wrongs done to them, or thought to be done to them, and for which they did not think they could get redress in Ireland itself. But some of them were from Irish plaintiffs, and there are several indications that the number of these increased throughout the reign and that their right of access to the Queen or her Privy Council (usually after dispensing appropriate douceurs to minor officials) was considered a valuable safety valve.

The Queen herself was the main target for Irish suitors, but she did not easily tolerate too many of them for long. She complained to the Privy Council in March, 1587, of being "at this time and always greatly charged with the suitors of that realm." [43] Many of the Old English and some of the Irish complainants at this time were men who had suffered losses in the Munster rebellion or in the plantation which followed. Sir John Perrot, then Lord Deputy, was instructed that in future he was to keep such suitors at home and must do better in settling Irish grievances for himself.[44] It may be that this limitation had some effect, as there are no complaints for several years. However, the Privy Council reacted strongly against what must have been a new wave of suitors in 1592, mentioning once more "the multitude of Irish suitors that do repair hither upon very slight occasion." [45] Most of them were described as recusants, and it is a reflection of the hardening of religious differences that the Clerk of the Council was now instructed to secure from Irish suitors the taking of the oath of allegiance and a certificate that they had been to church before bringing their suits before the Council. This, if rigidly enforced, was sufficient to deny to most Irish suitors any redress at English hands.

Barnaby Rich had himself been a suitor for Irish causes at Queen Elizabeth's Court and had little good fortune there. In *Greene's News* (1593) he asks, "What might be the cause that there is no more regard to the dispatching of poor suitors that have labored and tired themselves many ways in hope to have here a speedy release, as well for the redress of their sustained wrongs as also to be rewarded as they shall be found worthy by desert?" [46] The answer he found in bureaucratic delays and corruption. But looking back long afterward, he thought that the late Queen had after all been too generous to her Irish suitors and that they had not repaid her for her kindness:

How many gentlemen . . . of that country birth came daily into England about suits [he said] that were still begging and craving, and were continually returned from her Majesty's court back again into Ireland, laden with gifts and preferments that she graciously and liberally bestowed on them; who after they had passed and possessed their grants would never come in place to say "Amen," when they heard her Majesty prayed for, but that rather, by their ill example of contempt, made others more obstinate and stubborn than otherwise they would. [47]

But here he was asking even more than the Privy Council, that the Irish should conform in church after, as well as before, their suits were heard.

The Tudor fear of their own poor subjects, the attack on the beggars, the fear of the masterless (unemployed) man, can be

seen when Richard Beacon (in 1594) recommends their re-
moval from England to colonize Ireland—"The people poor and
seditious, which were a burden to the commonweal, are drawn
forth, whereby the matter of sedition is removed out of the
city"[48]—the equation between poverty and subversion being explicitly emphasized. There were many other proposals to export
the English poor to Ireland, America, or elsewhere: a statute of
1598 even conferred authority on officials to do so forcibly.[49] It
is not surprising therefore that unemployed and begging Irish
were regarded not only as pests to be removed from England
but as peculiarly dangerous ones. They were both poor, and so
potentially a disruptive element, and also Catholics who might
infect Englishmen. They were, too, after English relations with
Spain deteriorated, possible agents in Spanish plots against the
Queen and so were frequently regarded as enemies of the state.

Some Irishmen—they were as likely to come from Old English as purely Irish families—fell into the net in England because they were agents of the Counter-Reformation Catholic
Church. Christopher Roche, an Irishman of Washford [possibly
Waterford, rather than Wexford] was put in the stocks in London in 1592 "for speaking seditious words against the Queen's
Majesty," but he was not released when his punishment was
over, as he was suspected of being a priest. After more than a
year in jail he was formally interrogated. He then admitted he
had spent some time at the seminary towns of Reims and Douai,
where Catholic missionaries were trained. He refused to come to
church, and he was returned to prison with "a very dangerous
fellow" as the comment of the commissioners on his deposi-
tion.[50]

In 1593 and 1594 there were more serious apprehensions at
Court of Irish actions than any hitherto. In 1593 the Spaniards
discharged from their service in the Low Countries a number of
the seven hundred Irish and Old English soldiers who had deserted from the English to the Spaniards under Sir William

Stanley in 1587.[51] In March, customs officials were told to look out for and seize any such Irishmen as they might identify who should attempt to land in England.[52] An early group of these men, when examined, insisted they were not penniless or friendless and that they were all willing to serve the Queen once again. But at the beginning of 1594 more sinister information came to light. Hugh Cahill of Tipperary confessed that Sir William Stanley and others had arranged to employ "a tall, resolute, and desperate Irishman" to kill the Queen.[53] It is clear that Cahill, John Daniell, and Patrick Cullen were all involved in the plot, for which Cullen was after executed, while another Irishman, John Annias, closely associated with them, went to the Tower for a plot to kill Antonio Pérez, the refugee Spanish politician. Pérez wrote after the execution of Cullen and Annias: "Being in London, I chanced to be walking near the gate of the city in the neighborhood of St. Paul's at the time when they hoisted the heads above the gate." [54]

As the evidence of these desperate adventures was coming to light, precautionary measures against the Irish in general were taken under a proclamation of February 21, 1594 [55] (Plate 22). This begins by complaining that in and around London "there do haunt and repair . . . a great multitude of wandering persons." Of these, it went on, "some are men of Ireland that have of late years unnaturally served as rebels against her Majesty's forces beyond the seas, who cannot have any good meaning toward her Majesty, as of late hath been manifestly proved in some already taken, that have secretly come into the realm with full purpose, with procurement of the devil and his ministers, her Majesty's enemies, . . . to endanger her Majesty's noble person." Such men were to be arrested wherever they were found and proceeded against as traitors. But, it was argued, they could scarcely be easily identified "where there are also many other like vagrant persons of that nation that haunt about the Court by pretense only of suits, where they have no just

158

cause to make any." General regulations are therefore made: "No manner of person born in the realm of Ireland . . . shall remain in the realm but shall without delay repair into the realm of Ireland to the places of their natural habitation, where they ought to live, upon pain of imprisonment and punishment as vagabonds," while Englishmen who frequented the Court without cause were also to keep away from it. Four groups of Irishmen were exempted: "a householder known in some town where he liveth in the obedience of her Majesty's laws, a menial servant with some nobleman, gentleman, or some other honest householder," anyone "who does reside, or be in commons in any house of court or chancery, as a student in the laws or a student in any of the universities," or, finally, any persons "sent out of Ireland by her Majesty's deputy or some governors of the provinces there with commendation, or about any service or suit recommended." These make up the acceptable Irish element in the English population: all others are vagrants before the law, to whom must be applied the law of settlement, that is, their enforced return to their place of origin, where, the proclamation had said, "they ought to live."

Whether or not it was enforced fully, this proclamation laid down a coherent policy toward the Irish in England. That it was not fully enforced, so far as suits were concerned at least, is shown as early as 1596–1597, when there were fresh complaints of the importunity of suitors from Ireland who have troubled the Queen with their clamor.[56]

The last few years of the reign are too much taken up with fighting in Ireland to leave much room for dealing with the Irish in England. One incident shows graphically how active a part they might still play in the Irish wars. Three Dublin merchants were found in 1597 to be running an extensive business in supplying arms and other military equipment to the Earl of Tyrone.[57] Irish agents were buying swords and daggers from cutlers in Manchester and Birmingham and packing muskets and calivers, bought in London, for export to Ireland. Large quantities of lead were being sent from Liverpool and Chester, with muskets, morions, headpieces, swords, and daggers. How far this business was political or whether it was mainly commercial we do not know, but it illustrated some of the dangers an Irish element in the population might present to an English government that was attempting to complete the conquest of Ireland.

One consequence of the increased coming and going between Ireland and England was that, in English minds, the distinction, if it had ever been a clear one, between the Old English and the Irish from Ireland had become blurred, and that every man from Ireland was regarded as somewhat outlandish and expected to speak, like many of the Welsh who also came to Elizabethan England, an unintelligible tongue. This was especially galling to the Old English, who, while in Ireland, regarded themselves as very different from the Irish but, when they reached England, were thought of simply as Irishmen. Richard Stanyhurst is probably reflecting the indignities he himself suffered traveling as a student from Dublin to Oxford in 1563 when he complains that the English "judge them [the Old English] to learn their English in three or four days, as though they had bought at Chester a groat's worth of English and so packed up the rest to be carried after them to London." [58] Lord Howth was asked by Queen Elizabeth in 1562 whether he could speak the English tongue, his sarcastic comment being, "Such was the report of the country made to the Queen." [59]

The Cheshire men who rescued three Irish sailors from a storm-battered Dublin bark near Hilbre Island in 1561 were surprised that the men "could not speak English" and had some considerable difficulty in making themselves understood by them.[60] But Dr. Bartley has produced evidence that by 1603 a number of Irish words were known to London playgoers, as well as Irish usages of English, which suggests close contacts

The Irishman Translated

with Irishmen in England as well as in Ireland.[61] The anonymous play on Captain Thomas Stukely [62] published in 1605, but going back to 1596 or before, contained many Irish words and expressions, mingled with Irish-spoken English. Most curiously, it had an alternative version of one scene, one with much Irish in it, the other pruned for less accustomed ears of almost all "difficult" words. This suggests that some performances of the play may have been given to audiences in England which had an appreciable knowledge of Irish, or included a substantial number of Irishmen. Indeed, dramatists scarcely wrote without a demand for their wares, and there seems to have been a steady demand for Irishmen, wild or comic or both, on the Elizabethan stage. J. O. Bartley lists ten plays containing Irish characters first performed between 1588 and 1605 and amongst them the anonymous *Stukeley* and *Sir John Oldcastle* (1599), as well as Dekker's *Honest Whore*, Part II (ca. 1605), which showed more than a nodding acquaintance with the Irish language, as well as some more detailed acquaintance with Irish usages of English. Shakespeare's Captain Mackmorrice is a well-defined characterization of an Irish professional soldier, excitable, proud, extravagant in language. When Fluellen says something which sounds derogatory about his "nation," he rounds on him touchily—"Ish a villain, and a bastard, and a knave, and a rascal," [63] showing that his loyalties to the English Crown do not submerge his own.

The wild Irishman had thus, by the end of the Elizabethan period, come to town, and especially to London. He was known, both in the streets and on the stage, and in the process was losing, in English eyes, something of his wildness, becoming, if not readily assimilated, a commonly accepted part of the forcibly joined kingdoms of Great Britain and Ireland.

Appendix

Thomas Gainsford on Ireland

THOMAS GAINSFORD was a soldier in the Irish wars against Hugh O Neill and served under the Earl of Clanrickard at the battle of Kinsale in 1601. He did not publicize his experiences of Ireland until much later, his life of Hugh O Neill, *The True Exemplary, and Remarkable History of the Earle of Tirone,* appearing only in 1619. Earlier, in 1618, he had brought out *The Glory of England,* composed largely of eulogy of his native land but containing also topographical accounts of other countries, so that against their defects the advantages of England might be measured. His book proved popular, three editions being called for between 1618 and 1622. The section on Ireland (pp. 144–152), here reprinted in modernized form, is a good example of an Elizabethan's treatment of Ireland and the Irish. It is clear that he had read Camden's *Britannia* and Holinshed's *Chronicles* on Ireland, though it is not certain that he used Fynes Moryson's *Itinerary* (1617). Yet his impression of Ireland is an individual one, and, inside a framework of social description which by 1618 had become traditional, he adds many vivid touches from personal experience. The Irish are of lively interest to him: at the same time, by the primitiveness of their way of life they show up the superiority of the Englishman.

Appendix

The Description of Ireland

The country and kingdom of Ireland is generally for natural air and commodity of blessings sufficient to satisfy a covetous or curious appetite but withal divided into such fastness of mountain, bog, and wood that it hath emboldened the inhabitants to presume on hereditary security as if disobedience had a protection. For the mountains deny any carriages but by great industry and strength of men (so have we drawn the cannon over the deepest bogs and stoniest hills), and the passages are every way dangerous both for unfirmness of ground and the lurking rebel, who will plash down whole trees over the paces and so intricately wind them or lay them that they shall be a strong barricado, and then lurk in ambush amongst the standing wood, playing upon all comers as they intend to go along. On the bog they likewise presume with a naked celerity to come as near our foot and horse as is possible, and then fly off again, knowing we cannot, or indeed dare not, follow them: and thus they serve us in the narrow entrances into their glens and stony paths, or, if you will, dangerous quagmires of their mountains, where a hundred shot shall rebate the hasty approach of five hundred; and a few muskets (if they durst carry any), well placed, will stagger a pretty army, not acquainted with the terror or unpreventing the mischief.

The province of Leinster is more orderly than the rest, as being reasonable well inhabited and having some form of a commonwealth; so that I find no mislike either for delight or profit but that the want of wood abridgeth their computation of happiness, yet questionless was the principal cause of our reducing them to civility, and the place wherein we first settled many English families. Some unite and some divide the kingdom of Meath from Leinster and make it a province of itself containing East Meath, West Meath, and Longford, wherein O Roorck is resident, supposing himself the greatest gentleman in the world;

yea, contesting many times with Oneal, however with much ado he afforded him precedency. The country is very fruitful and pleasant, not so mountainous, but ill inhabited. For the wars, and their own bestiality, have not only made a separation of all good order but even terrified both beast and fowl from commorance [sojourning] amongst them in many places.

The province of Munster hath some towns well advanced by the seacoasts and many excellent harbors, wherein Ireland may boast over all the countries of Europe. The grounds adjacent are very fertile and in many places afford cause of ostentation, but more inward they are very barren and mountainous, full of bogs, wood, and other remote places, whose fastness hath incited the people to overgreat presumption. Yet because of the spaciousness, with men desiring good order, it might be reduced and reformed as enjoying plentiful and sweet rivers, full of fish, and some of sufficient depth to transport reasonable boats into the land.

The province of Connacht is divided from the rest by a goodly river called the Shannon, being, as I take it, the greatest of any island in the world, for it fetcheth a course of two hundred mile and filleth his channel along the shores of Longford, Meaths, Ormond, Limerick, and Kerry, yet serveth them in no great stead. For their shipping cometh no further than Limerick, where it is five mile broad fresh water and sixty mile from the main sea; from thence small cotts, as they term their boats, carry their wood, turf, fish, and other commodities; but for fish, as salmon, bream, pike, and divers other sorts, I shall not be believed to relate the numbers and hugeness by such as are enemies to observation or the belief of the blessings of other countries. Within twenty mile of Limerick, as I take it, a little beyond the precinct of Caher Castle [either at Castleconnell or Killaloe] a strange rock hath taken her lodging even cross [across] the river and filleth the room in such a manner that almost the navigation is hindered thereby. But what cannot men and money do? And why should not these idle people be industriously employed to remove the same and so free the passage to Athlone? As for an objection of impossibility, the judgment of men hath yielded to survey, and many examples have confirmed the effects of more laborious attempts. The south part, namely Thomond (for by reason of the river's interposing itself I see no reason why it should be disjointed from Connacht), with Galway and Clanrickard, is very stony, full of marble, alabaster, and jet, and hath better order both for number and good building in their castles than other parts of Ireland. The north from Athlone to the abbey of Aboile [Boyle], and so beyond the Curlewes as far as Sligo, is of excellent temperature and goodness. These Curlewes are mountains full of dangerous passages, especially when the kern take a stomach and a pride to enter into action, as they term their rebellion and tumultuary insurrections. On the other side the county of Mayo consorteth with the pleasingest place in the kingdom, by whose beaten banks lie those famous "Islands of Life," of whom a ridiculous tale is fathered that nothing dies in them, so that when the inhabitants grow old they are carried elsewhere, which custom they have of late superstitiously observed both in these islands of Aran and some other adjoining of the same condition, as they suppose.

The province of Ulster, and called the North, is very large and withal mountainous, full of great loughs of fresh water, except Lough Cone [Strangford Lough], which ebbeth and floweth as the sea shouldereth aside the straits at Strangford and with that violence at the ebb that a ship under sail with a reasonable gale of wind cannot enter against the tide. These lakes nature hath appointed instead of rivers and stored with fish, especially trout and pike, of such strange proportion that if I should tell you of a trout taken up in Tyrone forty-six inches long, and presented to the Lord Mountjoy, then Deputy, you would demand whether I was *oculatus testis,* and I answer, I ate my part of it, and as I take it both my Lord Davers and Sir William Godolphin were at the table, and worthy Sir Josias Bodley hath the portraiture depicted *in plano*. Here are no towns, or at least very few, but divers castles dispersed, and the inhabitants remove their cabins as their cattle change pasture, somewhat like the Tartarians, except in times of war and troubles. Then do they retire under the covert of castles and order their houses wonde [round?] with rods and covered with turfs, as well as they can, bringing their cattle even within their houses, lying altogether in one room, both to prevent robberies of kern and spoil by wolves. Amongst these every country is subject to the law "Tanist," which is, he which is best able to maintain the reputation of their family is the great "O" and commander.

Through the kingdom generally the winter is neither so cold nor the summer so hot as in England, by reason whereof harvest is very late, and in the North wheat will not quickly ripen, nor have they acorns once in a dozen year[s]. Their principal corn is oats, which are commonly burnt out of the straw and then trod from the husks with men's feet; of this they make their bread in cakes, being first ground by calliots [*cailleacha*, old women] and drudges very naked and beastly sitting on the ground with the mill like our mustard querns between their legs, and then upon broad iron presses they bake the meal when it is kneaded; which custom the best observe in Munster with their chiefest corn. The continual showers and mists make the country more dangerous to our nation, debarring the absolute assurance of wholesome air and the consequent health; seldom any frost continues or snow lieth long but on the mountains, in which are great store of deer both red and fallow. The abundance of wolves compels them to house their cattle in the bawns of their castles, where all the winter nights they stand up to the bellies in dirt; another reason is, to prevent thieves and falsehearted brethren, who have spies abroad and will come thirty miles out of one province into another to practice a cunning robbery.

The people are generally haters of bondage and beyond

measure proud; so that the younger brothers and
are as dear as the other, scorn all endeavors but l⌐
The gentlewomen stomach and, in truth, viliper
ers who get their living by trade, merchandise, ⌐
Yet are divers gravers in gold and silver called pₙ₋
who make their chalices, harps, buttons for their sleeves, crucifixes, and suchlike, in estimation amongst them. Their noblemen or lords (called dynasts) are known by "O" and "Mac,"
[the surname alone distinguishing the ruler, e.g., Ó Néill—the
O Neill—rather than Aodh Ó Néill—Hugh O Neill] and every
family hath such as minister justice to the people, famoused by
the title of Brehons, and yet the exactions over their tenants by
way of cuttings and other terrible impositions have caused
divers rebellions and insurrections amongst themselves, which
when the state hath attempted to reform, then have they stood
on their guard and taken indirect occasions to condemn our
usurpation, whereby their odious and hateful repinings, like a
menstruous cloth, have made their disobedience loathsome and
brought upon them such miseries as a calamitous war and angry
prince inflicteth turbulent people withal. These families have
also such as by way of history elate them to exorbitant actions,
joining withal the abuse of poetry and the deceit of physic,
known by the name of Bards, on whom depend certain harpers,
rhymers, and priests, which live in a kindred, the father instruct-
ing the son or brother, and he his cousin or friend. The name of
galloglass is in a manner extinct, but of kern in great reputation,
as serving them in their revolts and proving sufficient soldiers,
but excellent for skirmish.

They have strong and able bodies, proud hearts, pestilent
wits, liberal of life, subject to incontinency, amorous (wherein
their women are extraordinarily pleased), patient to endure,
lovers of music and hospitality, constant to their maintainers,
whether men or women, implacable in their hatred, light of belief, covetous of glory, impatient of reproach or contumely; not

thinking it yet any disgrace to receive a nickname at their chris-
tening, as "Con Oneale banco" [Conn Bacach Ó Néill, lame Con
O Neill] because he was lame. Besides, they are all extremely
superstitious, as indeed barbarous people are best observers of
ceremonies, and when any of them enters into religion it is admirable with what austerity they reform themselves. Their children are nursed abroad, and their foster fathers and foster
mothers are as dear to them as their own kindred. They use in-
cantations and spells, wearing girdles of women's hair and locks
of their lovers; they suppose idleness a glory of nature and by
their sluttish, or rather savage, customs strive to scorn (as they
say) our superfluity.

They are ready upon any enforcement by the imposturing art
of their Bards to innovation, as envying our first conquest and
stomaching they were never able to expel us. They are desperate
in revenge, and their kern think no man dead until his head be
off. They suppose theft no great offense, as imitating the Lace-
demonians, for they pray to prosper in their attempts; but these
be commonly the bastards of priests, who prove notorious vil-
lains, and the daughters either beg or become strumpets, or, if
you will, beggarly strumpets. They commonly intermix oaths
with their speeches, as "By the Trinity," "God," "His Saints," "St.
Patrick," "St. Brigid," "Faith," and "Troth," "The Temple," "Your
hand," "O Neal's hand," and suchlike.

Their marriages are strange, for they are made sometimes so
conditionally that upon a slight occasion the man taketh another
wife, the wife another husband. They are easily delivered of
their children,* and, if they have any by divers men, at their
deaths they resign them to the right father; the new married and
conceived with child giveth the Bard her best clothes.

They have soft and excellent skins and hands, but the small of
their legs hangeth in a manner over their brogues. Their apparel

* I have known of them delivered in the morning, and march along
with us the same day.

168

is a mantle to sleep in, and that on the ground on some rushes or flags; a thick gathered smock with wide sleeves graced with bracelets and crucifixes about their necks. They wear linen rolls about their heads of divers fashions; in Ulster carelessly wound about; in Connacht like bishops' miters, a very stately attire and once prohibited by statute; in Munster resembling a thick Cheshire cheese. Their smocks are saffroned against vermin, for they wear them three months together, but to be lousy is hereditary with the best of them and no disgrace.

Both men and women not long since accustomed a savage manner of diet, which was raw flesh, drinking the blood; now they seethe it and quaff up the liquor and then take "Usquebath." Not having flesh, they feed on watercresses, shamrocks, and "Bonniclaboch [*bainne clabair*]," which is milk strangely put into a tub a-souring, till it be clodded and curded together. When the cow will not let her milk down they blow her behind very strangely and sometimes thrust up their arms to their elbows, speaking words of gentleness and entreaty by way of bemoaning.

The men wear trouses, mantle, and a cap of steel. They are curious about their horses, tending to witchcraft; they have no saddles, but strange-fashioned pads; their horses are for the most part unshod behind; they use axes, staves, broadswords, and darts. In Terconnell [Tirconnaill] the hair of their head grows so long and curled that they go bareheaded and are called "Glibs" [*Glibeanna*, having locks of hair hanging over the eyes], the women "Glibbins" [*Glíbíni*, long-haired]. These and many other do the mere Irish observe with resolution and our wonderment not to be diverted, as if the poet should find fault with

> *Quo semel est imbuta recens servabit odorem*
> *Testa diu.*

Notes

CHAPTER I, pp. 1–6

1. Historical Manuscripts Commission, *Pepys MSS.* (London, 1911), p. 87.

CHAPTER II, pp. 7–13

1. Translated from *Catalogue of Irish Manuscripts in the Royal Irish Academy*, in Rev. Canice Mooney, "The Irish Church in the Sixteenth Century," *Proceedings of the Irish Catholic Historical Committee, 1962* (Dublin, 1963), p. 11.

2. James Spedding *et al.*, *The Letters and the Life of Francis Bacon*, III (London, 1868), 50.

3. T. Wright, *The passions of the minde* (1601), sig. A4.

CHAPTER III, pp. 14–19

1. Emyr Estyn Evans, "Atlantic Europe, the Pastoral Heritage," Fraser Lecture, University of Liverpool, 1962, which I was privileged to see in typescript; see also his *Irish Folk Ways* (London, 1956).

2. See Gerald A. Hayes-McCoy, "Gaelic Society in Ireland in the Late Sixteenth Century," *Historical Studies*, IV (London, 1963), ed. G. A. Hayes-McCoy, 45–61, the best brief account of Irish society in this period.

3. See also G. A. Hayes-McCoy, *Scots Mercenary Forces in Ireland, 1565–1603* (London, 1937), which includes an account of Irish society in this period, emphasizing its military aspects.

4. See D. A. Binchy, "Secular Institutions," in *Early Irish Society*, ed. Myles Dillon (Dublin, 1954), pp. 52–65; "The Linguistic and Historical Value of the Irish Law Tracts," in *Proceedings of the British Academy*, XXIX (1943), 195–228; "Lawyers and Chroniclers," in *Seven Centuries*

of Irish Learning, 1000–1700, ed. Brian Ó Cuiv (Dublin, 1961), pp. 58–71.

5. See Eleanor Knott, *Irish Classical Poetry* (2d ed., Dublin, 1960).

6. David Greene, "The Professional Poets," in *Seven Centuries of Irish Learning,* pp. 45–57.

7. Francis Shaw, "Irish Medical Men and Philosophers," in *Seven Centuries of Irish Learning,* pp. 87–101.

CHAPTER IV, pp. 20–33

1. Edward M. Hinton, *Ireland through Tudor Eyes* (Philadelphia, 1935), provides the only introductory survey.

2. Roger Hutchinson, *The image of God* (1550), in *Works* (Cambridge, 1842), p. 73.

3. George Turberville, *Tragicall Tales* (1587), sig. 2B1; reprinted in Richard Hakluyt, *Principall Navigations* (1589), p. 413.

4. Hakluyt, *Principall Navigations* (1589), pp. 388–389.

5. *Ibid.,* p. 112.

6. *A briefe and true report of the new found land of Virginia* (1588), sig. D3; D. B. Quinn, *The Roanoke Voyages* (Cambridge, 1955), I, 360–361.

7. Samuel Purchas, *Pilgrimes* (1625), IV, viii, 1647; XVIII (1906), 304.

8. *Ibid.,* p. 1655; XVIII (1906), 326.

9. John Smith, *Works,* ed. Edward Arber (Birmingham, 1884), p. lxvii.

10. *Ibid.,* pp. 102, 405.

11. Samuel Champlain, *Voyages* (Paris, 1619), sig. 84v–85r; *Les voyages de Samuel Champlain,* ed. Hubert Deschamps (Paris, 1951), p. 227.

12. *The Historie of Travell into Virginia Britania,* ed. Louis B. Wright and Virginia Freund (London, 1953), p. 71.

13. *Ibid.,* p. 73.

14. *Ibid.,* p. 79.

15. *Ibid.,* p. 114.

16. [George Mourt, ed.], *A relation . . . of the English Plantation setled at Plimouth* (London, 1622), p. 34; *Coming of the Pilgrim Fathers,* ed. Edward Arber (London, 1893), p. 453.

17. *New Englands prospect* (1634), p. 65.

18. *Ibid.*

19. *Ibid.,* p. 68.

20. *Ibid.,* p. 71.

21. Thomas Morton, *The New English Canaan* (Amsterdam, 1637), pp. 24, 25, 29–30; reprinted in "Publications of the Prince Society," XIV (Boston, 1883), ed. C. F. Adams, pp. 134–135, 143. The 1632 edition has not been seen.

22. Richard Jobson, *The Golden Trade* (1623), pp. 36–37.

23. *Ibid.,* p. 71.

24. *Ibid.,* p. 105.

25. Matthew Parker, *Correspondence,* ed. John Bruce and T. T. Perowne (Cambridge, 1833), p. 123.

26. *Calendar of State Papers, Spanish, 1587–1603* (London, 1899), pp. 656–657.

27. Gervase Markham, "The Newe Metamorphosis," British Museum, Department of Manuscripts, Additional MS. 14824, fo. 19v.

28. *An Itinerary* (London, 1617); 4 vols. (Glasgow, 1907–1908); additional matter in *Shakespeare's Europe,* ed. Charles Hughes (London, 1903). Most of the Irish matter, with further additions, is collected in Caesar Litton Falkiner, *Illustrations of Irish History* (London, 1904), pp. 211–325. (The first item is abbreviated below *Itin.*)

29. William Nicolson, *The English, Scotch and Irish Historical Libraries* (London, 1736), "The Irish Historical Library," p. 4, thought this "somewhat probable," and a similar view is expressed by Thompson Cooper in the article on William Good in the *Dictionary of National Biography.* The case is strengthened until it is almost conclusive (and Camden's treatment of his Irish section in successive editions is clarified) by Rudolf B. Gottfried, "The Early Development of the Section on Ireland in Camden's *Britannia," ELH,* X (1943), 17–30. I am indebted to Dr. F. J. Levy for help on this problem.

30. *Britain, or a Chorographicall Description of . . . England, Scotland, and Ireland,* trans. Philemon Holland (London, 1610), 2d pagination, pp. 142–148. (Abbreviated below *Brit.*)

31. His "Description of Ireland" appeared in Raphael Holinshed, *Chronicles* (London, 1577), vol. I, pt. iii, sigs. A1r–[D4v]; 2d ed. (London, 1587), vol. II, sigs. [A5r]–[D5r]; 3d ed. (6 vols., London, 1807–1808), vol. VI, pp. 1–69. His *De rebus in Hibernia gestis* (Antwerp, 1584) is an independent work which has not been translated. For Stanyhurst see St. John D. Seymour, *Anglo-Irish Literature, 1200–1582* (Cambridge, 1929), pp. 145–165. (The first item hereafter cited as *Chron.*)

32. Edmund Campion, "Historie of Ireland," in *The Historie of Ireland, Collected by Three Learned Authors,* ed. Sir James Ware (Dublin, 1633), pp. 13–20; reprinted as *A Historie of Ireland (1571),* with an introduction by Rudolf B. Gottfried (New York, 1940). These have now been superseded by *Two Bokes of the Histories of Ireland,* ed. A. F. Vossen (Assen, 1963), which also contains an admirable study of Campion as a historian.

33. "Ireland, Elizabeth I and the Counter-Reformation," in *Elizabethan Government and Society,* ed. S. T. Bindoff *et al.* (London, 1961), pp. 323–326.

34. *A view,* ed. Sir James Ware (1633)—hereafter cited as *View,* from *A View,* ed. W. L. Renwick (London, 1934)—and *Prose Works (Variorum Spenser,* ed. Edwin A. Greenlaw *et al.,* vol. IX), ed. Rudolf B. Gottfried (Baltimore, 1949), pp. 43–231.

35. See Thomas M. Cranfill and Dorothy Hart Bruce, *Barnaby Rich* (Austin, 1953)—although his Irish career is not covered wholly satisfactorily.

36. Sig. B1.

37. Most of his Irish papers are in *Nugae Antiquae*, II (London, 1779). See also *Letters and Epigrams*, ed. Norman E. McClure (Philadelphia, 1930), and "A Short View of the State of Ireland Written in 1605," *Anecdota Bodleiana*, no. 1, ed. William Dunn Macray (Oxford, 1879). A good brief sketch of his life is in Sir John Harington, *A New Discourse of a Stale Subject, Called the Metamorphosis of Ajax*, ed. Elizabeth Story Donno (New York and London, 1962), pp. 1–10.

CHAPTER V, pp. 34–57

1. *State Papers, Henry VIII,* II (London, 1830), 1.

2. C. L. Falkiner, *Illustrations* (1904), p. 311; cf. pp. 242, 245–246.

3. Irish Manuscripts Commission, *Analecta Hibernica,* no. 2 (Dublin, 1931), p. 95.

4. Huntington Library, Ellesmere MSS., EL 1701 (September, 1573).

5. Public Record Office, London, State Papers, Ireland, Elizabeth, S.P. 63/42, 74 (Nov. 6, 1573); *Calendar of State Papers, Ireland, 1509–1573* (London, 1860), p. 528.

6. P.R.O., S.P. 63/195, 18; *Calendar of State Papers, Ireland, 1596–1597* (London, 1893), pp. 162–163.

7. P.R.O., S.P. 63/274, 62 (1); see John Dawtrey, *The Falstaff Saga* (London, 1927), pp. 191–192; *Calendar of State Papers, Ireland, 1594–1596* (London, 1890), p. 247.

8. *View,* ed. Renwick, p. 45; *Prose Works,* p. 79.

9. Falkiner, *Illustrations,* p. 246.

10. *Calendar of Carew Manuscripts, 1575–1588* (London, 1868), p. 43.

11. See especially *Historical Studies,* IV (1963), ed. G. A. Hayes-McCoy, 54–58.

12. Falkiner, *Illustrations,* pp. 311–312.

13. *Ibid.,* p. 311.

14. *Chron.* (1577), I, iii, D3r–[D4r]; VI (1808), 67.

15. Camden, *Brit.* (1610), 2d pagination, p. 148.

16. *The fyrst boke of the introduction of knowledge* [1548?], sig. C4r–C4v; ed. F. J. Furnivall (London, 1870), p. 131.

17. Falkiner, *Illustrations,* pp. 248–249; cf. Camden, *Brit.* (1610), 2d pagination, p. 144.

18. *Chron.* (1577), I, iii, [D4r]; VI (1808), 68.

19. Falkiner, *Illustrations,* p. 284.

20. *Chron.* (1577), I, iii, [D4r]; VI (1808), 68.

21. *Ibid.*
22. Huntington Library, Ellesmere MSS., EL 1701.
23. Dublin, National Library of Ireland, MS. 669, fo. 11.
24. *Chron.* (1577), I, iii, [D4r]; VI (1808), 68.
25. Falkiner, *Illustrations,* pp. 286–287.
26. *View,* ed. Renwick, p. 98; *Prose Works,* p. 127.
27. *Chron.* (1577), I, iii, [D4r]; VI (1808), 68.
28. Dublin, National Library of Ireland, MS. 669, fo. 11.
29. *View,* ed. Renwick, pp. 93–94; *Prose Works,* pp. 123–124.
30. Falkiner, *Illustrations,* p. 287.
31. Camden, *Brit.* (1610), 2d pagination, p. 147.
32. Falkiner, *Illustrations,* p. 248; cf. p. 311.
33. *Chron.* (1577), I, iii, [D4r]; VI (1808), 67.
34. *View,* ed. Renwick, p. 94; *Prose Works,* p. 124.
35. Camden, *Brit.* (1610), 2d pagination, p. 144.
36. *Seven Centuries of Irish Learning,* ed. B. Ó Cuiv, pp. 50–51 (see also Eleanor Knott, *Irish Classical Poetry,* p. 9).
37. "Smyth's Information for Ireland," *Ulster Journal of Archaeology,* 1st ser., VI (Belfast, 1858), 166.
38. *Chron.* (1577), I, iii, [D4v]; VI (1808), 68.
39. *Ulster Journal of Archaeology,* 1st ser., VI, 167.
40. *The Bardic Poems of Tadhg Dall Ó Huiginn,* ed. and trans. Eleanor Knott (London, 1926), II, 5.
41. *Calendar of State Papers, Ireland, 1601–1603* (London, 1912), pp. 681–682; Russell K. Alspach, *Irish Poetry: From the English Invasion to 1798* (Philadelphia, 1959), p. 28.
42. Translated in Douglas Hyde, *Literary History of Ireland* (London, 1899), p. 473.
43. *The Life of Sir John Perrot* (London, 1728), pp. 11–12.
44. Daniel MacCarthy, *Life and Letters of Florence MacCarthy . . . Mor* (Dublin, 1867), p. 362.
45. Quoted in E. Knott, *Irish Classical Poetry,* p. 73.
46. *Chron.* (1577), I, iii, [D4v]; VI (1808), 68.
47. *Ulster Journal of Archaeology,* 1st ser., VI, 166.
48. *View,* ed. Renwick, p. 7; *Prose Works,* p. 47.
49. *Ulster Journal of Archaeology,* 1st ser., VI, 166.
50. Falkiner, *Illustrations,* p. 274.
51. *View,* ed. Renwick, p. 8; *Prose Works,* pp. 47–48.
52. *Ulster Journal of Archaeology,* 1st ser., VI, 166.
53. *Chron.* (1577), I, iii, [D4v]; VI (1808), 68.
54. Camden, *Brit.* (1610), 2d pagination, p. 144.
55. *Ulster Journal of Archaeology,* 1st ser., VI, 166–167.
56. *Seven Centuries of Irish Learning,* ed. B. Ó Cuiv, p. 49.
57. *Ulster Journal of Archaeology,* 1st ser., VI, 166–167.
58. Hippocrates, *Aphorismi:* many sixteenth-century editions.

59. D. *Justiniani institutionum libri IV:* many sixteenth-century editions.

60. *Chron.* (1577), I, iii, [D4v]; VI (1808), 68.

61. *Seven Centuries of Irish Learning,* ed. B. Ó Cuiv, pp. 91–95.

62. *Itin.* (1617), III, iii, 159; IV (1908), 192; Falkiner, *Illustrations,* p. 221.

63. P.R.O., S.P. 63/13, 36; *Calendar of State Papers, Ireland, 1509–1573,* p. 299; S.P. 63/34, 45; *Calendar,* p. 462. See *Calendar of Dublin Records,* ed. Sir John Gilbert, II (Dublin, 1891), xiv–xv.

64. Camden, *Brit.* (1610), 2d pagination, p. 144. See also Stanyhurst in *Chron.* (1577), I, iii, [D4r]; VI (1808), 67.

65. *Chron.* (1577), I, iii, [D4v]; VI (1808), 68.

66. *Itin.* (1617), III, iii, 164; IV (1908), 202–203; Falkiner, *Illustrations,* pp. 232, 245.

67. *Chron.* (1577), I, iii, [D4r]; VI (1808), 67.

68. *A New Description of Ireland* (1610), pp. 34–40.

69. *Calendar of State Papers, Ireland, 1588–1592* (London, 1885), p. 203, and *Calendar of Carew Manuscripts, 1589–1600* (London, 1869), pp. 71–72.

70. Falkiner, *Illustrations,* p. 245.

71. *Ibid.*

72. John Dymmok, "A Treatice of Ireland," in Irish Archaeological Society, *Tracts Relating to Ireland,* II (Dublin, 1843), no. 1, pp. 8–9; cf. National Library of Ireland, MS. 669; *View,* ed. Renwick, pp. 44–45; *Prose Works,* pp. 78–79.

73. Dublin, National Library of Ireland, MS. 669.

74. "A Treatice," p. 9.

75. *View,* ed. Renwick, p. 64–65; *Prose Works,* pp. 97–98.

76. *View,* ed. Renwick, pp. 98–99; *Prose Works,* pp. 127–128.

77. Falkiner, *Illustrations,* p. 322; cf. p. 248.

78. *View,* ed. Renwick, p. 99; *Prose Works,* p. 128.

79. Falkiner, *Illustrations,* p. 248; *View,* ed. Renwick, pp. 99–100, 206; *Prose Works,* pp. 127–128, 219.

80. *Calendar of Patent and Close Rolls, Ireland, Henry VIII–Elizabeth,* I (Dublin, 1861), 485–487.

81. Philip Sidney, *Works,* ed. Albert Feuillerat, III (Cambridge, 1923), 49–50.

82. *Chron.* (1577), I, iii, A3r; VI (1808), 5.

CHAPTER VI, pp. 58–61

1. *A letter sent by I. B. Gentleman unto his very frende Mayster R. C. Esquire* (London, [1571?]), sig. D1.

2. *A briefe description of Ireland made in 1589* (London, 1589 and 1590), sig. A3; reprinted in Irish Archaeological Society, *Tracts Relating to Ireland,* I (Dublin, 1841), no. 2.

3. "A Newe Metamorphosis," British Museum, Additional MS. 14829, book ii, fo. 25r&v.

4. See Alexander C. Judson, *Spenser in Southern Ireland* (Bloomington, 1933) and *The Life of Edmund Spenser* (Baltimore, 1945).

5. *Faerie Queene*, VII, VI, xxxviii, liv–lv; *Variorum Spenser*, VI (1938), 161, 165.

CHAPTER VII, pp. 62–90

1. *The Image of Irelande, with a discoverie of Woodkarne* (London, 1581), sig. A4v; facsimile, ed. John Small (Edinburgh, 1883), p. 8.

2. P.R.O., S.P. 63/46, 26 (May 20, 1574); *Calendar of State Papers, Ireland, 1574–1585* (London, 1867), p. 24.

3. Rich, *A New Description* (1610), p. 40.

4. *Itin.* (1617), III, iii, 163; IV (1908), 199; Falkiner, *Illustrations*, p. 229.

5. Emyr Estyn Evans, *Irish Folk Ways* (London, 1956), p. 81.

6. *Itin.* (1617), III, iii, 161; IV (1908), 197; Falkiner, *Illustrations*, p. 226.

7. *Ibid.*

8. *Itin.* (1617), III, iii, 163; IV (1908), 199; Falkiner, *Illustrations*, p. 229.

9. *Ibid.*

10. Hugh Allingham, *Captain Cuellar's Adventures in Connaught and Ulster, A.D. 1588* (Belfast, 1897), p. 55.

11. *Itin.* (1617), III, iii, 163; IV (1908), 200, 201; Falkiner, *Illustrations*, pp. 229–230, 321.

12. *A New Description* (1610), p. 25.

13. Falkiner, *Illustrations*, p. 321. Cf. *Itin.* (1617), III, iii, 163; IV (1908), 201.

14. *Chron.* (1577), I, iii, [D4r]; VI (1808), 67; Camden, *Brit.* (1610), 2d pagination, p. 148.

15. Falkiner, *Illustrations*, p. 321. Cf. *Itin.* III, iii, 162; IV (1908), 198–199.

16. *Itin.* (1617), III, iii, 163; IV (1908), 200; Falkiner, *Illustrations*, p. 230.

17. Falkiner, *Illustrations*, pp. 320, 249. Cf. *Itin.* III, iii, 161; IV (1908), 195.

18. Falkiner, *Illustrations*, pp. 323–324.

19. *Itin.* (1617), III, iii, 162; IV (1908), 199; Falkiner, *Illustrations*, pp. 228–230.

20. *Itin.* (1617), III, iii, 162, 163; IV (1908), 198–199, 201; Falkiner, *Illustrations*, pp. 228, 230.

21. *Chron.* (1577), I, iii, [D4r]; VI (1808), 67.
22. *Itin.* (1617), III, iii, 162; IV (1908), 198; Falkiner, *Illustrations,* p. 228.
23. *Itin.* (1617), III, iii, 163, 162; IV (1908), 201, 199; Falkiner, *Illustrations,* pp. 230, 228.
24. *Itin.* (1617), III, iii, 163; IV (1908), 200; Falkiner, *Illustrations,* pp. 229-230.
25. Falkiner, *Illustrations,* pp. 320-321.
26. *Itin.* (1617), III, iii, 163; IV (1908), 200; Falkiner, *Illustrations,* p. 229.
27. Camden, *Brit.* (1610), 2d pagination, p. 147.
28. *Chron.* (1577), I, iii, [D4r]; VI (1808), 67.
29. Falkiner, *Illustrations,* p. 361.
30. *Itin.* (1617), III, iii, 162; IV (1908), 197; Falkiner, *Illustrations,* p. 227.
31. Falkiner, *Illustrations,* p. 338.
32. *Itin.* (1617), III, iii, 162; IV (1908), 197, 198; Falkiner, *Illustrations,* p. 227.
33. Camden, *Brit.* (1610), 2d pagination, p. 148.
34. *Chron.* (1577), I, iii, [D4r], 4; VI (1808), 67, 8.
35. *Aqua Vitae,* published by the Dolmen Press.
36. *A New Description* (1610), p. 24.
37. *Itin.* (1617), III, iii, 162; IV (1908), 198; Falkiner, *Illustrations,* p. 228.
38. *A New Description* (1610), p. 27.
39. *The fyrst boke of the introduction of knowledge,* sig. C3; ed. F. J. Furnivall, p. 131.
40. E. Topsell, *The History of Four-Footed Beasts . . . Whereunto is now added, the Theater of Insects; . . . by T. Moffet. . . . Revised by J. R[owland]* (London, 1658), II, 1092.
41. Sig. P8; ed. Huntington Brown (Cambridge, Mass., 1937), p. 121.
42. *Itin.* (1617), III, iv, 180; IV (1908), 236-237.
43. *View,* ed. Renwick, p. 69; *Prose Works,* p. 102.
44. *Itin.* (1617), III, iv, 180; IV (1908), 236.
45. E. E. Evans, *Irish Folk Ways,* pp. 33-38.
46. *Itin.* (1617), III, iii, 164; IV (1908), 202; Falkiner, *Illustrations,* pp. 231-232.
47. See E. E. Evans, *Irish Folk Ways,* pp. 86-87.
48. *Itin.* (1617), III, iii, 164; IV (1908), 202; Falkiner, *Illustrations,* p. 231. Cf. III, iv, 181; IV (1908), 238.
49. P.R.O., S.P. 63/79, 55; *Calendar of State Papers, Ireland, 1574-1585* (London, 1867), p. 278. See Spenser, *View,* ed. Renwick, p. 279.
50. *Itin.* (1617), III, iv, 180-181; IV (1908), 237-238. Jaroslav z Donína succeeded his father in 1597 and was later abbot of Nová Celle.

The family, known in Czech as Donín and elsewhere as Dohna, Dhona, etc., had large estates in Bohemia, Silesia, and other parts of Central Europe. No systematic record of his travels is known (*Ottuv Slovník naucný*, VII, 835; for the reference to which, as for other assistance, I am indebted to Professor Otakar Odlozilik, University of Pennsylvania).

51. See Joseph Raftery, *Prehistoric Ireland* (London, 1951), pp. 29–34; *Historical Studies*, IV (1963), ed. G. A. Hayes-McCoy, 58.

52. Harold G. Leask, *Irish Castles and Castellated Houses* (Dundalk, 1941), pp. 75–112; cf. Sidney Toy, *The Castles of Great Britain* (2d ed., London, 1954), pp. 217–231.

53. Leask, *Irish Castles*, pp. 116–117.

54. Richard Stanyhurst, *De rebus in Hibernia gestis* (1584), pp. 32–33. The quotation has been translated from Stanyhurst's original Latin.

55. *Itin.* (1617), III, ii, 74; III (1908), 498.

56. Stanyhurst, *De rebus*, p. 33.

57. *Itin.* (1617), III, ii, 74; III (1908), 498–499.

58. *Itin.* (1617), III, iii, 160; IV (1908), 193; Falkiner, *Illustrations*, p. 222.

59. *Bardic Poems*, ed. E. Knott, II, 24.

60. Falkiner, *Illustrations*, pp. 360–361.

61. *Ibid.*, pp. 248–250.

62. *View*, ed. Renwick, p. 203; *Prose Works*, p. 217.

63. Falkiner, *Illustrations*, p. 250.

64. Camden, *Brit.* (1610), 2d pagination, pp. 143–144.

65. *A New Description* (1610), p. 36.

66. *View*, ed. Renwick, p. 79; *Prose Works*, p. 111.

67. *View*, ed. Renwick, p. 180; *Prose Works*, pp. 196–197.

68. Falkiner, *Illustrations*, pp. 249–250.

69. E. E. Evans, *Irish Folk Ways*, pp. 3, 129–131.

70. *A New Description* (1610), p. 26.

71. Falkiner, *Illustrations*, p. 322; see also p. 263.

72. *Itin.* (1617), III, iii, 163; IV (1908), 201; Falkiner, *Illustrations*, p. 230.

73. Camden, *Brit.* (1610), 2d pagination, p. 143.

74. *Chron.* (1577), I, iii, [D4r]; VI (1808), 67.

75. Falkiner, *Illustrations*, p. 245.

76. E.g., Smyth in *Ulster Journal of Archaeology*, 1st ser., VI, 167.

77. Rev. Canice Mooney, "The Irish Church in the Sixteenth Century," *Proceedings of the Irish Catholic Historical Committee, 1962*, p. 6; cf. Falkiner, *Illustrations*, p. 319.

78. Camden, *Brit.* (1610), 2d pagination, p. 145.

79. *Chron.* (1577), I, iii, [D4v]; VI (1808), 68–69.

80. *Calendar of Carew Manuscripts, 1575–1588*, p. 284.

81. Falkiner, *Illustrations*, p. 284.

82. *Ibid.*
83. *Ulster Journal of Archaeology,* 1st ser., VI, 167.
84. *View,* ed. Renwick, p. 69; *Prose Works,* pp. 101–102.
85. Falkiner, *Illustrations,* p. 318; see also p. 315.
86. Falkiner, *Illustrations,* p. 320.
87. Camden, *Brit.* (1610), 2d pagination, p. 147.
88. *View,* ed. Renwick, pp. 72–73; *Prose Works,* p. 105.
89. *Chron.* (1577), I, iii, [D4r]; VI (1808), 67.
90. *The Irish hubbub* (1617), sig. B2.
91. *Works,* ed. J. Spedding *et al.,* VI (London, 1858), 471.
92. *Works* (London, 1625), p. 398.
93. Falkiner, *Illustrations,* p. 318; cf. p. 261.
94. *Two Bokes of the Histories of Ireland* (1963), p. [25] (second pagination).
95. *View,* ed. Renwick, p. 88; *Prose Works,* p. 119.
96. "A Survey of the Present State of Ireland" (1615), Huntington Library, Ellesmere MS., EL 1746, fo. 11v.
97. Camden, *Brit.* (1610), 2d pagination, p. 148; also Stanyhurst in *Chron.* (1577), I, iii, [D4v]; VI (1808), 69.
98. Falkiner, *Illustrations,* p. 314.
99. *A New Description* (1610), pp. 25–27.
100. *Calendar of State Papers, Ireland, 1601–1603,* p. 687.
101. Camden, *Brit.* (1610), 2d pagination, p. 147; Falkiner, *Illustrations,* p. 314.
102. Camden, *Brit.* (1610), 2d pagination, pp. 145–148.
103. *The fyrst boke of the introduction of knowledge,* sig. C4r–C4v; ed. F. J. Furnivall, pp. 133–135.
104. See *Calendar of State Papers, Ireland, 1601–1603,* where they are briefly calendared, pp. 661–687.
105. *Two Bokes of the Histories of Ireland* (1963), pp. [5]–[6], [17].
106. Falkiner, *Illustrations,* p. 317. Though Lady Essex wrote to Southampton on May 13, 1599: "Pray commend me to Sir Harry Davers, and bid him take heed of the saffron smocks. I think he means not to write to any of his friends till he may write in Irish, which is more eloquent than the English"; Historical Manuscripts Commission, *Salisbury MSS.,* IX (London, 1902), 166, cited in A. L. Rowse, *Shakespeare's Southampton* (London, 1965), p. 139.
107. *Calendar of State Papers, Ireland, 1598–1599* (London, 1895), p. 440.
108. *Chron.* (1577), I, iii, A3v; VI (1808), 6.
109. *View,* ed. Renwick, p. 87; *Prose Works,* p. 118.
110. Falkiner, *Illustrations,* p. 262.
111. *Calendar of State Papers, Ireland, 1598–1599,* p. 440; see also Falkiner, *Illustrations,* p. 244.

112. Camden, *Brit.* (1610), 2d pagination, p. 142.
113. *Chron.* (1577), I, iii, [D4r]; VI (1808), 67.
114. Dublin, National Library of Ireland, MS. 669; and see John Dymmok, "A Treatice," in Irish Archaeological Society, *Tracts,* II, 6.
115. "A Short View," *Anecdota Bodleiana* (1879), p. 9.

CHAPTER VIII, pp. 91–105

1. This chapter is largely based, though with some differing interpretation, on Henry F. McClintock, *Old Irish and Highland Dress* (2d ed., Dundalk, 1950); see also A. S. Henshall and W. A. Seaby, "The Dungiven Costume," *Ulster Journal of Archaeology,* 3d ser., XXIV–XXV (Belfast, 1963), 119–143.
2. Camden, *Brit.* (1610), 2d pagination, p. 148.
3. *View,* ed. Renwick, pp. 65–70; *Prose Works,* pp. 99–102.
4. *Itin.* (1617), III, iv, 180; IV (1908), 236.
5. Camden, *Brit.* (1610), 2d pagination, p. 148.
6. *View,* ed. Renwick, p. 79; *Prose Works,* p. 111; *Itin.* (1617), III, iv, 180; IV (1908), 236; see also Campion, *Hist.* (1633), p. 24.
7. *Itin.* (1617), III, iv, 180; IV (1908), 236. Cf. *Itin.* (1617), III, iii, 160; IV (1908), 194; Falkiner, *Illustrations,* p. 223
8. *Chron.* (1577), I, iii, [D4r]; VI (1808), 67.
9. *View,* ed. Renwick, pp. 65, 69, 74, 79; *Prose Works,* pp. 99, 102, 106, 110–111.
10. Translated by Kenneth J. Jackson, *A Celtic Miscellany* (London, 1951), pp. 236–237.
11. *Faerie Queene,* V, XII, xiv; *Variorum Spenser,* V (1936), 145.
12. See A. M. Hind, "Studies in English Engraving," *The Connoisseur,* XCI (London, 1933), 230.
13. Lucas de Heere, "Corte beschryuinghe van Engheland, Schotland ende Irland," British Museum, Additional MS. 28330; "Theatre de tous les peuples de la terre avec leurs habits," Ghent, University Library MS. 2466. Daniel Rogers in 1575 proposed to publish the *Topographia* of Gerald of Wales with "the pictures of the Irish costumes," which may have been those drawn by De Heere; see J. A. van Dorsten, *Poets, Patrons and Professors* (Rotterdam, 1962), pp. 22–23.
14. See T. M. Chotzen and A. M. E. Draak, *Beschrijving der Britsche Eilanden* (Antwerp, 1937), pp. 37–39, translated by H. F. McClintock as "A Sixteenth Century Dutch 'Account of Ireland,'" *Journal of the Royal Society of Antiquaries of Ireland,* LXIX (Dublin, 1939), 223–225.
15. Camden, *Brit.* (1610), 2d pagination, p. 148.
16. *View,* ed. Renwick, p. 69; *Prose Works,* p. 101.
17. *The Theatre of the Empire of Great Britaine* (1611), p. 138.
18. Camden, *Brit.* (1610), 2d pagination, p. 148.

Notes, pages 95–107

19. *Itin.* (1617), III, iv, 180; IV (1908), 237.
20. Camden, *Brit.* (1610), 2d pagination, p. 148.
21. *Chron.* (1577), I, iii, [D4r]; VI (1808), 67.
22. *Itin.* (1617), III, iv, 180; IV (1908), 237.
23. *Calendar of State Papers, Ireland, 1588–1592*, pp. 192–193.
24. P.R.O., S.P. 63/45, 60 (II).
25. British Museum, Cotton MSS., Augustus, I, 38–39.
26. Dublin, Trinity College MS. 1209, no. 13.
27. Hakluyt, *Principall Navigations* (1589), p. 492.
28. Falkiner, *Illustrations*, p. 284.
29. *Ibid.*, p. 360.
30. Huntington Library, MS. HM 25863.
31. *The Image of Irelande, with a discoverie of Woodkarne*, sig. E1v; facsimile, p. 46.
32. Fiant 1440, in *11th Report of the Deputy Keeper of the Records of Ireland* (Dublin, 1879), app. 5, p. 215.
33. Historical Manuscripts Commission, *De l'Isle and Dudley MSS.*, II (London, 1934), 242, 272 (2), 455, 491, 500, 519, 521, 536, 537 (2), 539 (2), 570.
34. *The Image of Irelande*, sig. D1v; facsimile, p. 38.
35. *Itin.* (1617), III, iv, 180; IV (1908), 236–237. Cf. Falkiner, *Illustrations*, pp. 261, 321.
36. *Letters and Epigrams*, ed. N. E. McClure (1938), p. 78.
37. *The Image of Irelande*, sig. B2; facsimile, p. 11.
38. Cf. *Historical Studies*, IV (1963), ed. G. A. Hayes-McCoy, 58.
39. *Calendar of State Papers, Ireland, 1598–1599*, p. 440; cf. Falkiner, *Illustrations*, pp. 321–322.
40. *The fyrst boke of the introduction of knowledge*, sig. C3; ed. F. J. Furnivall, pp. 131–132.
41. *Ibid.*, sig, C3v; ed. F. J. Furnivall, pp. 132–133.
42. *The Image of Irelande*, sig. F1v; facsimile, p. 54.
43. *Ibid.*, sig. F2; facsimile, p. 55.
44. *Ibid.*, sig. F2r&v; facsimile, pp. 55–56.
45. A. S. Henshall and W. A. Seaby, "The Dungiven Costume," *Ulster Journal of Archaeology*, 3d ser., XXIV–XXV, 119–142, plates XIII–XVI.

CHAPTER IX, pp. 106–122

1. See D. B. Quinn, "Ireland and Sixteenth Century European Expansion," in *Historical Studies*, I (1958), ed. T. Desmond Williams, 26–27; E. P. Cheyney, "Some English Conditions Surrounding the Settlement of Virginia," in *American Historical Review*, XII (1906–1907), 507–528; H. M. Jones, *O Strange New World* (New York, 1964), pp. 167–179.
2. *Calendar of State Papers, Ireland, 1509–1573*, p. 318.

181

3. D. B. Quinn, *The Voyages and Colonising Enterprises of Sir Humphrey Gilbert* (London, 1940), I, 8–14.

4. D. B. Quinn, "Sir Thomas Smith (1509–1577) and the Beginnings of English Colonial Theory," *Proceedings of the American Philosophical Society*, LXXXVIII (Philadelphia, 1944), 543–560; Mary Dewar, *Sir Thomas Smith: A Tudor Intellectual in Office* (London, 1964), pp. 156–170; *Irish Historical Studies*, XIV (1965), 285–287.

5. Historical Manuscripts Commission, *De l'Isle and Dudley MSS.*, II, 12–15.

6. Oxford, Bodleian Library, Carte MS. 56 (vol. I), p. 57.

7. See Alfred Leslie Rowse, *Sir Richard Grenville* (London, 1937), pp. 64–70.

8. Quinn, *Gilbert*, I, 14–19.

9. *Calendar of State Papers, Ireland, 1509–1573*, pp. 406, 428.

10. Robert Dunlop, "Sixteenth Century Schemes for the Plantation of Ulster," *Scottish Historical Review*, 1st ser., XXII (Glasgow, 1924–1925), 124–126, 199–212.

11. Thomas Churchyard, *A generall rehearsall of warres* (1579), sig. F1 (a copy in the Folger Library alone has the date); *Calendar of State Papers, Ireland, 1509–1573*, pp. 514, 521, 523; D. B. Quinn, "Simão Fernandes, a Portuguese Pilot in the English Service, circa 1573–1588," *Congresso Internacional de Historia dos Descobrimentos, Actas*, III (Lisbon, 1961), 451–452.

12. *Calendar of State Papers, Ireland, 1574–1585*, p. 77 (July 31, 1575); Richard Bagwell, *Ireland under the Tudors*, II (London, 1885), 301–302.

13. Historical Manuscripts Commission, *De l'Isle and Dudley MSS.*, I (London, 1925), 411–412.

14. Oxford, Bodleian Library, Carte MS. 56 (vol. I), p. 82 (Feb. 2, 1573); *Calendar of State Papers, Ireland, 1574–1585*, pp. 225, 255–256.

15. Quinn, "Simão Fernandes," pp. 452–454.

16. Edward Edwards, *Life and Letters of Sir Walter Ralegh*, II (London, 1868), 3–4; P.R.O., S.P. 63/96, 30, 31; *Calendar of State Papers, Ireland, 1574–1585*, p. 406.

17. *Works*, ed. Albert Feuillerat, III (1923), 46–50.

18. Quinn, *Gilbert*, II, *passim*.

19. Quinn, *Gilbert*, I, 84.

20. Quinn, *Gilbert*, I, 94–95; *Calendar of State Papers, Ireland, 1574–1585*, pp. 524–526, 529–530, 537, 540, 548, 551, 568, 571, 585. There is internal evidence that Carleill collaborated with Edward Hayes in 1592 or 1593 in a plan to colonize North America (Cambridge University MS. Dd. 3. 85, no. 4). In November, 1593, he was spoken of as recently dead (T. Birch, *Memoirs of the Reign of Queen Elizabeth* [1754], I, 130).

21. D. B. Quinn, *The Roanoke Voyages, 1584–1590* (London, 1955), I, 287–288.

22. Alfred Leslie Rowse, *Sir Richard Grenville*, pp. 267–286; "Sir Richard Grenville's Place in English History," *Proceedings of the British Academy*, XLIII (Oxford, 1957), 93–94.

23. Quinn, *Roanoke Voyages*, I, 64, 74; II, 500, 519–520, 541, 770, 776–777, 834–838 (Darby Glande); II, 506, 520, 835 (Dennis Carroll).

24. Sir Richard Grenville—P.R.O., S.P. 63/28, 39 (misplaced in *Calendar of State Papers, Ireland, 1509–1573*, p. 409); Sir Walter Raleigh—*Calendar of State Papers, Ireland, 1588–1592*, pp. 170–172.

25. *Calendar of State Papers, Ireland, 1588–1592*, p. 171.

26. Quinn, *Roanoke Voyages*, I, 321.

27. P. H. Hulton and D. B. Quinn, eds., *The American Drawings of John White* (1964), I, 21.

28. *Calendar of State Papers, Ireland, 1598–1599*, pp. 326, 324.

29. *An answere . . . to a fraudulent letter of M. George Blackwels* (1602), sig. ¶4v–A1.

30. *Calendar of Carew Manuscripts, 1601–1603* (London, 1870), p. 462.

31. P.R.O., C.O. 1/1, 9—a corrupt text with some doubtful readings.

32. *Calendar of State Papers, Ireland, 1601–1603*, pp. 315–319.

33. Falkiner, *Illustrations*, p. 298.

34. *Calendar of State Papers, Ireland, 1598–1599*, pp. 138–139, 156. The employment of a number in the Netherlands, "for the better quiet of this state," had already been planned in 1582 (Public Record Office of Ireland, Calendar of the Council Book, 1581–1586, p. 74).

35. *Calendar of State Papers, Ireland, 1600* (London, 1903), p. 401.

36. *Calendar of State Papers, Ireland, 1600–1601* (London, 1905), p. 305; see also *Itin.* (1617), II, ii, 100; II (1907), 379.

37. Irish Manuscripts Commission, *Analecta Hibernica*, no. 4 (Dublin, 1932), pp. 157–158.

38. Alexander Brown, *The Genesis of the United States* (New York, 1890), I, 198.

39. *Calendar of State Papers, Ireland, 1603–1606* (London, 1872), pp. 325–326.

40. Historical Manuscripts Commission, *Downshire MSS.*, II (London, 1936), 258.

41. *Ibid.*, p. 406.

42. Library of Memorial University, St. John's, Newfoundland.

43. Historical Manuscripts Commission, *Hastings MSS.*, IV (London, 1947), 160.

44. See James Spedding *et al.*, *The Letters and the Life of Francis Bacon*, IV (London, 1868), 123.

45. *Ibid.*, VII (London, 1874), 175.
46. Richard Whitbourne, *A Discourse Containing a Loving Invitation* (1622), sig. A4.
47. *Itin.* (1617), III, iii, 156; IV (1908), 185.

CHAPTER X, pp. 123–142

1. British Museum, Harleian MS. 35, fo. 195.
2. See *Historical Studies*, I (1958), ed. T. Desmond Williams, 8–9.
3. P.R.O., S.P. 63/49, 78; *Calendar of State Papers, Ireland, 1574–1585*, p. 54.
4. Historical Manuscripts Commission, *Salisbury MSS.*, II (London, 1888), 309.
5. P.R.O., S.P. 63/43, 27; *Calendar of State Papers, Ireland, 1509–1573*, p. 535.
6. P.R.O., S.P. 63/41, 43; *Calendar of State Papers, Ireland, 1509–1573*, p. 514.
7. *A generall rehearsall of warres*, sig. D2v.
8. See *Historical Studies*, I (1958), ed. T. Desmond Williams, 28.
9. Quinn, *Gilbert*, I, 16–17; Churchyard, *A generall rehearsall of warres*, sig. Q1–R1.
10. *Ibid.*, sig. 2E1r&v.
11. P.R.O., S.P. 63/41, 76 (II); *Calendar of State Papers, Ireland, 1509–1573*, p. 517.
12. P.R.O., S.P. 63/41, 2; *Calendar of State Papers, Ireland, 1509–1573*, p. 508.
13. *A Discoverie of the True Causes why Ireland was Never entirely Subdued* (1612), p. 165.
14. *Letters and Memorials of State*, ed. Arthur Collins (London, 1746), I, 108.
15. *Ibid.*, pp. 78, 108.
16. Historical Manuscripts Commission, *Salisbury MSS.*, II, 421.
17. *View*, ed. Renwick, pp. 136–142; *Prose Works*, pp. 159–163.
18. P.R.O., S.P. 63/46, 15; *Calendar of State Papers, Ireland, 1574–1585*, p. 23.
19. *Chron.* (1587), II, [R1v]–[R2r]; VI (1808), 460.
20. *View*, ed. Renwick, p. 135; *Prose Works*, p. 158.
21. Northamptonshire Record Office, Fitzwilliam Papers, no. 66, fo. 9v.
22. *Solon His Follie* (Oxford, 1594), sig. ¶3–¶4v.
23. *Ibid.*, sig. M2, B4v.
24. Lord Deputy and Council to Privy Council, *Calendar of State Papers, Ireland, 1596–1597*, p. 250.
25. Historical Manuscripts Commission, *Salisbury MSS.*, IX, 302.

26. Historical Manuscripts Commission, *Salisbury MSS.*, X (London, 1904), 345.

27. *Calendar of State Papers, Ireland, 1599–1600* (London, 1900), p. 334.

28. British Museum, Additional MS. 14824, fo. 21.

29. T. P., *Englands hope against Irish hate* (1600); unique copy in Lambeth Palace Library.

30. R[ichard] V[enner], *Englands joy* [London?, 1601?]. (STC 21358, as, mistakenly, by Richard Verstegen.)

31. In Humfrey Dyson, *A book containing all such proclamations as were published during the raigne of Queen Elizabeth*, no. 361.

32. *Itin.* (1617), II, i, 51; II (1907), 273.

33. *Itin.* (1617), II, ii, 138; II (1907), 461.

34. *Itin.* (1617), II, iii, 268; III (1908), 275–276.

35. *Itin.* (1617), II, iii, 270; III (1908), 278–279.

36. *Calendar of State Papers, Ireland, 1599–1600*, p. 306.

37. *Calendar of State Papers, Ireland, 1598–1599*, p. 209.

38. *Itin.* (1617), II, iii, 211; III (1908), 152.

39. "Chroniculary Discourses," in "William Farmer's Chronicles of Ireland," ed. C. L. Falkiner, *English Historical Review*, XXII (1907), 129–130.

40. *Itin.* (1617), II, iii, 271–272; III (1908), 282–283.

41. *A Heart Full of Thought* (Dublin, 1959), p. 11.

42. *Calendar of Carew MSS., 1603–1624* (London, 1873), pp. 305–310.

CHAPTER XI, pp. 143–161

1. See *Calendar of the Bristol Apprentice Book, 1532–1542*, ed. D. Hollis, "Bristol Record Society Publications," vol. XIV (Bristol, 1949).

2. *Annals of Ulster*, ed. W. M. Hennessey and B. MacCarthy, III (Dublin, 1895), 49; Henry Ellis, *Original Letters*, 1st ser., I (London, 1824), 186.

3. R. Gruffyth to Wolsey. *Letters and Papers, Henry VIII*, IV, ii (London, 1872), no. 4485.

4. Stephen ap Parry. *Letters and Papers, Henry VIII*, XI (London, 1888), no. 2, p. 2.

5. *The copye of the submissyon of Oneyll* (1542).

6. *A treatyse of the newe India*, in E. Arber, ed., *The First Three English Books on America* (Birmingham, 1885), p. 9.

7. See J. O. Bartley, *Teague, Shenkin and Sawney* (Cork, 1954), pp. 26–27.

8. *Acts of the Privy Council, 1571–1575* (London, 1894), p. 88.

9. *Letters and Memorials of State*, ed. Arthur Collins (London, 1746), I, 133.

10. *Stationers' Register*, ed. Edward Arber, I, 287, 290.

11. Historical Manuscripts Commission, *Salisbury MSS.*, III (London, 1889), 113.

12. See Thomas Harman, *A Caveat or Warening For Commen Cursetors* (1567), sig. C4v.

13. *Ibid.*, sig. D2.

14. *Ibid.*, sig. G3.

15. *Ibid.*, sig. G2–G3.

16. *Calendar of State Papers, Domestic, 1581–1590* (London, 1865), p. 142.

17. *Acts of the Privy Council, 1591* (London, 1900), p. 280.

18. *Acts of the Privy Council, 1592* (London, 1901), pp. 99–100.

19. Thomas Dekker, *Works*, ed. R. H. Shepperd (London, 1873), II, 96; J. O. Bartley, *Teague, Shenkin and Sawney*, p. 8.

20. *Liverpool Town Books*, ed. J. A. Twemlow, I (Liverpool, 1918), 283.

21. Historical Manuscripts Commission, *Salisbury MSS.*, XII (London, 1910), 523, 637–638, 676.

22. W. R., *The most horrible and tragicall murther of . . . John Lord Bourgh, Baron of Castell Connell. Committed by Arnold Cosby* (1591).

23. *Calendar of State Papers, Ireland, 1509–1573*, pp. 162, 184.

24. *Liverpool Town Books*, ed. J. A. Twemlow, I, 220.

25. J. O. Bartley, *Teague, Shenkin and Sawney*, p. 11.

26. *Gabriel Harvey's Marginalia*, ed. G. C. Moore Smith (Stratford-upon-Avon, 1913), p. 194.

27. " 'A Discourse of Ireland' *circa* 1599," ed. D. B. Quinn, *Proceedings of the Royal Irish Academy*, XLVII (Dublin, 1942), sect. C., pp. 164–165.

28. J. O. Bartley, *Teague, Shenkin and Sawney*, pp. 13–14.

29. Anthony Chute, *Tobacco* (1595), sig. C2.

30. Falkiner, *Illustrations*, p. 315.

31. *History of Queen Elizabeth* (London, 1688), p. 62; see James Hogan, "Shane O'Neill Comes to the Court of Elizabeth," *Feílcríbhinn Torna*, ed. Séamus Pender (Cork, 1947), pp. 154–170.

32. Edmund Campion, *Two Bokes of the Histories of Ireland* (1963), p. [139].

33. *Diary of Henry Machyn*, ed. John Gough Nichols (London, 1848), pp. 274–275, 277.

34. *Calendar of State Papers, Ireland, 1509–1573*, p. 209; Historical Manuscripts Commission, *Pepys MSS.*, p. 14.

35. P.R.O., S.P. 12/51, 43; *Calendar of State Papers, Ireland, 1509–1573*, p. 198.

36. In *Certaine devises and shewes presented by the gentlemen of*

Grayes-Inne (1587); see J. O. Bartley, *Teague, Shenkin and Sawney*, p. 10.

37. *Stationers' Register*, ed. Edward Arber, II, 254.

38. See J. O. Bartley, *Teague, Shenkin and Sawney*, p. 9.

39. Historical Manuscripts Commission, *De l'Isle and Dudley MSS.*, I, 368.

40. Barnaby Rich's petition to the Queen. P.R.O., S.P. 63/144, 34; *Calendar of State Papers, Ireland, 1588–1592*, pp. 182–183.

41. Historical Manuscripts Commission, *Pepys MSS.*, p. 173.

42. Richard Bagwell, *Ireland under the Tudors*, III (1890), 216.

43. *Acts of the Privy Council, 1586–1587* (London, 1897), p. 373.

44. *Acts of the Privy Council, 1587–1588* (London, 1897), p. 211.

45. *Acts of the Privy Council, 1591–1592* (London, 1901), pp. 587–588.

46. STC 12259, attributed to Robert Greene.

47. *A New Description of Ireland* (1610), p. 22.

48. *Solon His Follie* (1594), sig. O3r&v.

49. 39 Elizabeth, cap. 3; *Statutes of the Realm*, IV (London, 1819), 896.

50. Huntington Library, Ellesmere MSS., EL 2128.

51. See Brendan Jennings, "Irish Swordsmen in Flanders, 1586–1610," *Studies*, XXXVI (Dublin, 1939), 402–410.

52. *Calendar of State Papers, Domestic, 1591–1594* (London, 1867), pp. 432–433.

53. Historical Manuscripts Commission, *Salisbury MSS.*, X, p. 58; *Calendar of State Papers, Domestic, 1591–1594*, pp. 436–438, 464–465, 484.

54. Gregorio Marañón, *Antonio Pérez* (London, 1954), pp. 317–319.

55. H. Dyson, *A book containing all such proclamations* (1618), no. 324.

56. *Calendar of State Papers, Ireland, 1596–1597*, p. 332.

57. *Ibid.*, pp. 318, 323.

58. *Chron.* (1577), I, iii, A3v; VI (1808), 6.

59. Cited in *Two Bokes of the Histories of Ireland*, pp. 58–59, from "Book of Howth" in *Calendar of Carew MSS.*, V (London, 1871), 201.

60. *Liverpool Town Books*, ed. J. A. Twemlow, I, 160–161.

61. J. O. Bartley, *Teague, Shenkin and Sawney*, pp. 7–13.

62. *The Famous Historye of the life and death of Captaine Thomas Stukeley.*

63. *Henry V*, III, ii, 127–128.

Suggested Reading

THERE are few brief accounts of Elizabethan Ireland which are worth reading. That in James Camlin Beckett, *A Short History of Ireland* (3d ed., London, 1959) is the best, while Edmund Curtis, *The History of Ireland* (London, 1938; reissued 1962) is also useful. The detailed narrative, pedestrian and narrow but reliable and informative, is Richard Bagwell, *Ireland under the Tudors* (3 vols., London, 1885–1890; reprinted 1962). More specialized matter can be traced through Conyers Read, *Bibliography of British History, Tudor Period, 1485–1603* (2d ed., Oxford, 1959). Monographs of special value are Robert Dudley Edwards, *Church and State in Tudor Ireland* (London, 1935); Gerald A. Hayes-McCoy, *Scots Mercenary Forces in Ireland (1565–1603)* (London, 1937); Cyril Falls, *Elizabeth's Irish Wars* (London, 1950); Ada K. Longfield, *Anglo-Irish Trade in the Sixteenth Century* (London, 1929). References to a number of detailed papers will be found in the footnotes. G. B. O'Connor, *Elizabethan Ireland, Native and English* (Dublin [1906]) is a useful elementary introduction, somewhat dated. Constantia E. Maxwell, *Irish History from Contemporary Sources (1509–1610)* (Dublin, 1923) and Caesar Litton Falkiner, *Illustrations of Irish History and Topography* (London, 1904) contain invaluable selections of contemporary materials. A. L. Rowse included two chapters on Ireland in *The Expansion of Elizabethan England* (London, 1955).

The background to Irish society can be studied in Emyr Estyn Evans, *Irish Folk Ways* (London, 1956); Joseph Raftery, *Prehistoric Ireland* (London, 1951); Sean Ó Suilibheann, *Handbook of Irish*

188

Suggested Reading

Folklore (Dublin, 1942); Harold G. Leask, *Irish Castles and Castellated Houses* (Dundalk, 1941).

Brief introductions to the literature and culture of Gaelic Ireland have been published by the Stationary Office, Dublin: *Early Irish Society*, ed. Myles Dillon (1954); *Seven Centuries of Irish Learning, 1000–1700*, ed. Brian Ó Cuiv (1961); Eleanor Knott, *Irish Classical Poetry* (2d ed., 1960). Douglas Hyde, *The Literary History of Ireland* (London, 1889) is still valuable, as is Robin Flower, *The Irish Tradition* (Oxford, 1947). An illuminating approach is that in Vivian Mercier, *The Irish Comic Tradition* (Oxford, 1962). Kenneth J. Jackson, *A Celtic Miscellany* (London, 1951) includes several translations from Irish writings of the sixteenth century, while detailed examples of Irish literature can be found in the original and in translation in *The Bardic Poems of Tadhg Dall Ó Huiginn*, ed. Eleanor Knott (2 vols., London, 1922–1926), and Lughaidh Ó Clerigh, *The Life of Aodh Ruadh Ó Domnaill*, ed. Paul Walsh and Colm Ó Lochlainn (2 vols., Dublin, 1948–1957).

For English writers and observers in Ireland there is only one general introduction, reliable but slight, in Edward M. Hinton, *Ireland through Tudor Eyes* (Philadelphia, 1935). There are detailed studies by Henry Robert Plomer and Tom Peete Cross, *The Life and Correspondence of Lodowick Bryskett* (Chicago, 1927); Thomas M. Cranfill and Dorothy Hart Bruce, *Barnaby Rich* (Austin, 1953), not entirely reliable on his Irish career; Pauline Henley, *Spenser in Ireland* (Cork, 1928); Alexander C. Judson, *The Life of Edmund Spenser* (Baltimore, 1945); Constantia E. Maxwell, *The Stranger in Ireland* (London, 1954); St. John D. Seymour, *Anglo-Irish Literature, 1200–1582* (Cambridge, 1929); Russell K. Alspach, *Irish Poetry: From the English Invasion to 1798* (2d ed., Philadelphia, 1959).

James Orr Bartley, *Teague, Shenkin and Sawney* (Cork, 1954) has a full discussion of Irish influences in English drama, while Henry Foster McClintock, *Old Irish and Highland Dress* (2d ed., Dundalk, 1950) gives an authoritative account of costume.

The principal texts by English visitors to Elizabethan Ireland may be found in: Andrew Boorde, *The Fyrst Boke of the Introduction of Knowledge* [1548?], ed. F. J. Furnivall for the Early English Text Society (London, 1870); Edmund Campion, *Two Bokes of the His-*

Suggested Reading

tories of Ireland, ed. A. F. Vossen (Assen, 1963), facsimile of 1633 edition, *A History of Ireland (1571),* ed. Rudolf B. Gottfried (New York, 1940); Richard Stanyhurst, "The Description of Ireland," in Raphael Holinshed, *Chronicles* (editions of 1577, 1587, 1808), *De rebus in Hibernia gestis* (Antwerp, 1584), not translated (Philip Ó Sullivan Beare attacked him for his alleged slanders on the Irish in *Zoilomastix,* ed. T. J. O'Donnell [Dublin, 1960]); Father Good's account of Ireland, in William Camden, *Britannia* (1607), translated by Philemon Holland as *Britain* (1610); Edmund Spenser, *A View of the Present State of Ireland*—the best editions are *Complete Works of Edmund Spenser,* ed. William L. Renwick, vol. IV (London, 1934), *Prose Works* in the *Variorum Spenser,* ed. Edwin A. Greenlaw *et al.,* vol. IX, ed. Rudolf B. Gottfried (Baltimore, 1949); Barnaby Rich, *A New Description of Ireland* (1610), and Richard Beacon, *Solon His Follie* (1594), no modern editions; Fynes Moryson, *An Itinerary* (1617) (4 vols., Glasgow, 1907–1908), supplemented in *Shakespeare's Europe,* ed. Charles Hughes (London, 1903), and in Caesar Litton Falkiner, *Illustrations of Irish History* (1904); John Dymmok, "A Treatice of Ireland," in Irish Archaeological Society, *Tracts Relating to Ireland,* vol. II (Dublin, 1843), no. 1; Sir John Harington, *Nugae Antiquae,* ed. Thomas Park (2 vols., London, 1804), and "A Short View of Ireland Written in Anno 1605," in *Anecdota Bodleiana,* ed. William Dunn Macray, no. 1 (Oxford, 1879); John Derricke, *The Image of Ireland* (1581), facsimile ed. John Small (Edinburgh, 1883); Thomas Gainsford, *The Glory of England* (1618), no modern edition, but the Irish section is reprinted as an Appendix to this monograph.

Index

Principal subject entries will be found under the Irish major headings

Index

Bowes, Sir Jerome, cited, 97–98
Boyle Abbey, Co. Roscommon, 165
Bradshaw, Rev. Lawrence, 149–150
Bregia, 74
Breitheamh, breitheamhain (brehon[s]), 17, 45
Bridewell (prison), London, 148
Bristol, 143, 144
British Isles, 7, 27, 60, 125
Britons, ancient, 74
Buaile, buailte (booley[s]), 14–15, 53
Buannacht (levy of food), 16
Buannacht bairr (free quarter at discretion), 52
Buannacht bheag (money levy), 52
Buannacht bhona (levy of victuals, 51
Bunratty Castle, Co. Clare, 73
Burghley, Lord, *see* Cecil, William, Lord Burghley
Burke, Richard, Earl of Clanrickard, 162
Burkes, 2
Butler, Michael, 113
Butler, Thomas, Earl of Ormond, 97, 99, 148, 149; cited, 146

Caher Castle, 164
Cahill, Hugh, 158
Cailleacha (old women), 25, 127, 166
Caiseal (stone-walled enclosure), 72
Calvina, a goddess, 59
Camden, William, 27, 28, 152, 162; cited, 153
Campion, Edmund, 21, 29, 84, 87–88; cited, 153
Caoine (to keen), 83
Cape Cod, 23
Carew, George, Lord, cited, 141
Carey, George, Lord Hunsdon, 135
Caribbean Sea, 110
"Carick Sidney" (ship), 111
Carleill, Christopher, 113, 182
Carolinas, 111

Carrigaline, Co. Cork, 109
Carrol, Dennis, 114
Castle Connell, Co. Limerick, 150, 164
Cathair (stone-walled enclosure), 72, 74
Cathay, 107
Cavan, Co., 121
Cavendish, Thomas, 153 n.
Cearrbhaigh (professional gamblers), 54
Cecil, Sir Robert, Earl of Salisbury, 12, 44, 71, 120, 135, 138, 139
Cecil, Sir Thomas, 125
Cecil, William, Lord Burghley, 62, 124, 126, 153; cited, 125
Ceithearn, ceithearnaigh (kern[s]), 16, 93
Champlain, Samuel de, 24
Charleville (Rath Luirc), Co. Cork, 115
Cheshire, 110, 160
Chester, 143, 149, 160; Bishop of, 150; Mayor of, 150
Chichester, Sir Arthur, Lord Deputy, 120–121, 139
China, 117, 153
Churchyard, Thomas, cited, 126–127, 127–128, 128–129
Chute, Anthony, cited, 152
Cios mhac an ríogh (king's son's services), 37
Cios ríogh (king's tribute), 37
Clandeboye, Ulster, 132
Clanrickard, Earl of, *see* Burke, Richard
Clanrickard, Co. Galway, 165
Clare, Co., 72, 73
Coinnmheadh (coyne), 52
Cóisireacht (feasting), 50
Coleraine, Co. Londonderry, 113
Condé, Prince of, 147
Cone, Lough, *see* Strangford Lough
Connacht, Province of, 2, 4, 6, 130, 133, 134; Composition of, 127; described, 36, 59–60, 129, 164–165, 169

192

Index

Index

Hariot, Thomas, 115, 116; cited, 23
Harman, Thomas, cited, 147, 148
Hartpole, Robert, 127
Harvey, Gabriel, cited, 151
Hayes, Edward, 182
Hayes-McCoy, Prof. Gerald A., cited, 32
Heere, Lucas de, drawings by, 91, 92, 93–94, 95, 96
Henry VII, 143
Henry VIII, 3, 19, 34, 93, 94, 144, 145
Herbert, Sir William, cited, 96–97
Hibernia (Bernia), 59
Hilbre Island, Cheshire, 160
Hippocrates, 18, 48
Holinshed, Raphael, 29, 162
Holmes, Giles, cited, 23
Hooker, John, 132
Howth, Lord, see St. Lawrence, Christopher
Hughes, Thomas, cited, 153–154
Hunsdon, Lord, see Carey, George
Hyde, Douglas, cited, 44

Iberia, 14
Indians, North American, 20, 23, 24, 25, 27, 116, 121; Algonkians, 23, 25, 115, 119, 153 n.
Inghean ríogh or *Inghean an ríogh* (king's daughter), 37
Irish artifacts
bagpipes, 41, 96
board (table), 103
boats, 164
chalices, 167
cotts, *see* boats
crucifixes, 167, 169
cushions, 103
dishes, 103
handmills, *see* querns
harps, 42, 167
linen cloth, 132; "linen" (shirts?), 101
metal vessels, 67
needles, long, 140
ovens, *see* presses
pipes, *see* bagpipes

plows, 77, 78, 79, 108, 128, 132, 133
presses (pot-ovens?), 166
querns, 63, 166
stirrup-cup, 75
table, *see* board
tankard, 103
Irish, culture traits attributed to
affected to vainglory, 37, 42, 89, 90, 167
bake bread in iron presses, 166
bathe in stone troughs, 79
bear children easily, 82, 168
believe souls of dead go to be with heroes, 87
burn oats from the straw, 63, 166
cattle raid a test of manhood, 46
cook in a hide, 66, 67, 102, 103
custom of taking and repudiating wives, 80, 81, 168
damp mantles for sleeping, 71
deathbed speeches tend to mirth, 83
drink at parting, 75
drink blood from cattle and horses, 65, 79, 169
eat flesh of animals that have died, 65
esteem foster brothers, 84, 85, 90
gamblers play for the members of their body, 54
grind corn naked, 63
hang in a withe, 83
harbor lice, 68, 69, 70
hospitality, 1, 75, 89, 90
induce milk in cows, 169
intermix oaths with their speech, 168
keen at a death, 24–25, 83
kill horses with long needles, 140
leave milk vessels unwashed, 64
lie in circle around fire, 70
lie on women's laps to have lice killed, 69
maintain concubines, 81, 83
maintain itinerant prostitutes, 69, 70, 82, 168

195

Index

Index

Index

Index

Index

Index

London, 71; Bishop of, 146; Lord
  Mayor of, 148; Tower of, 146,
  154, 158; Welsh in, 9, 13;
  Irish in, 99, 143, 145, 146,
  147, 148, 149, 150, 152, 153,
  154, 155, 156, 157, 158, 160,
  161
Londonderry, Co., 71, 105, 121
Longford, Co., 163, 164

"Mac," 138, 167
Mac an Bhaird, Laoiseach, cited,
  92
MacCab, 154
MacCarthy Mor, Florence, 44
Mac Cumhaill, Fionn, 87
MacDé, mac diabhail (God's son,
  Devil's son), 151
MacEntee, Maire, cited, 141
Mackmorrice, Captain, 161
Mac Oisín, Oscar, 87
Mac ríogh or Mac an ríogh (king's
  son), 37
MacSweeneys, 101–102
Maine, 113
Malbie, Nicholas, 127
Manchester, 118, 159
Mandeville, Sir John, 30
Manteo, 153 n.
Markham, Gervase, cited, 27, 59–
  60, 135–136
Mary I, Queen of England, 3, 4,
  106
Massachusetts, 25
Masterson, Thomas, 127
Mauvissière, Castelnau, Michel de,
  Seigneur de la, 147
Mayo, Co., 1, 165
Meath, Co., 2, 163, 164
Mexico, 21, 108
Milford, 143
Mná suibhail (wandering women),
  82
Moffet, Dr. Thomas, cited, 69
Molana Abbey, 115
Monaghan, Co., 5
Morton, Thomas, cited, 25
Moryson, Fynes, 27–28, 31, 40–41,
  45, 56, 67, 85; cited, 34–35,
37, 38, 39, 39–40, 41, 42, 46,
  48, 49–50, 51, 54, 55, 63, 64,
  65, 66, 67–68, 69, 70–71, 71–
  72, 73, 74, 76, 77, 78, 79, 81,
  82, 83, 84, 86, 88, 89, 91, 92,
  95, 98, 100, 101, 122, 138,
  139, 152
Mountjoy, Lord, see Blount,
  Charles
Mourt's Relation, cited, 24
Munster, Province of, 61, 81, 96,
  111; described, 164, 166, 169;
  Presidency Council in, 4, 30,
  55; English repression in,
  126–129, 132–133; plantations, 109, 112, 114, 115, 116,
  118, 133, 141, 155; rebellions,
  44, 109, 111, 116, 117, 132–
  133, 155

Netherlands (Low Countries), 27,
  119, 157, 183
New England, 23, 24, 25, 112
Newfoundland, 113, 121, 122
Newry, Co. Down, 140
Newtown, Co. Cork, 115, 119
Normans, 7, 8, 38, 107
North America, 23, 106, 111, 112,
  113, 114, 115, 182
North Carolina, 111, 113
North Carolina Algonkians, see
  Indians
Northwest Passage, 107, 112
Norumbega, 112, 115, 118
Norway, 14
Nová Celle, 177
Nova Scotia, 113

"O," 138, 167
O Briens of Thomond, 15, 73
O Cahan, Donnell, 64, 71–72, 105
O Cahan's country, Co. London-
  derry, 64; family of, 105
O Carroll of Ely O Carroll, 35
O Connor Faly, Brian, 146
O Connor Sligo, Sir Donough,
  154–155
O Connor Sligo, Owen, 154–155
O Connors of Offaly, 3

Index

Index

DATE DUE